The Scottish Railway Book

John Thomas

3 115794

DAVID & CHARLES
NEWTON ABBOT LONDON NORTH POMFRET (VT) VANCOUVER

ISBN 0 7153 7324 2

Library of Congress Catalog Card Number 76–54089

Photoset in 10 on 11 Times
printed and bound in Great Britain by
REDWOOD BURN LIMITED
Trowbridge & Esher
for David & Charles (Publishers) Limited
Brunel House Newton Abbot Devon

Published in the United States of America
by David & Charles Inc
North Pomfret Vermont 05053 USA

Published in Canada
by Douglas David & Charles Limited
1875 Welch Street North Vancouver BC

CONTENTS

PREFACE

The *Times Literary Supplement* described *Scottish Railway History in Pictures*, when it was published in 1967, as 'an unashamed exercise in Scottish railway nationalism.' My own description of the book in the introduction was 'a series of photographic essays on many aspects of Scottish railway life.' Anyway, my readers, especially my English readers, liked it and wrote to say so. The book set a new pattern in railway albums which has been imitated since.

In recent years potential readers have written to say that they cannot obtain *Scottish Railway History in Pictures* except at fancy prices in second-hand shops. My publisher and myself got our heads together to consider whether we should reprint the book. After careful deliberation we decided to produce a new type of album which would have much wider scope than the original in that it would include substantial text, a wide range of good visual documentary material and a fresh selection of pictures all blended to capture the feeling of Scottish railways. The result is *The Scottish Railway Book*.

JOHN THOMAS,
Glasgow, August 1976.

1 INTRODUCTION

In the early years of the nineteenth century, Scotland, to all but a handful of Englishmen, was as remote as New Zealand—or for that matter the moon. The stage coaches from London to Glasgow and Edinburgh could spend a fortnight on the journey and tickets cost a fortune. The alternative was an uncertain and often uncomfortable sea journey. People travelled only if they had to or if they were rich and adventurous. In 1803, when Dorothy and William Wordsworth discovered little-known Loch Lomond, they thought in terms of intrepid explorers setting foot for the first time on the shores of Lake Tanganyika. The railway was to change all that.

At first, even men of learning saw little future in the tramroads built to link collieries with rivers and canals, and the success of the Stockton & Darlington Railway in 1825 did little to alter their way of thinking. *Locomotion* had been at work for more than three years before George Stephenson publicly expressed his conviction that the new railways one day would link up to form a national network. But in 1824 a Scotsman had elaborated on the same theme in a pamphlet which had achieved international notice. He was Charles Maclaren, editor of *The Scotsman*, and in December 1824 he devoted the front page of four consecutive issues of his newspaper to the theme that railways, with the new steam engines running on them, would not only straddle Britain but girdle the world.

Once the idea of a long distance network was accepted railways came with a rush. By 1846 travellers from London could travel to Newcastle by train, continue by the *Quicksilver* coach to Berwick and there board the Edinburgh-bound trains on the North British Railway. The rail link through Northumberland to the south bank of the Tweed was completed on 1 July 1847 although it was not until 29 August 1850 that the English and Scottish systems were linked by the Royal Border Bridge. Meanwhile a second great trunk route had been built from London to Carlisle and the Caledonian Railway had taken it across the Border and on to Edinburgh and Glasgow by 15 February 1848. At last Scotland was open to the English masses.

On 1 August 1850 the Caledonian Railway ran a cheap excursion from Carlisle to Glasgow. The editorial which the *Carlisle Journal* saw fit to print the following day sheds light on the conditions faced by the pioneer Anglo-Scottish rail travellers:

> Yesterday morning at four o'clock a cheap excursion train started from Carlisle to Glasgow the object being to allow the passengers an opportunity of being present at the Highland and Agricultural Society's great show. The train consisted of twenty cattle trucks in which was strewn a plentiful supply of straw. The carriages were, of course, regular standups there being nothing in the shape of seats provided and the passengers were packed in like sheep. From Carlisle there were 96 passengers—not a very large number but it was considerably augmented by the time the train passed Beattock. People must indeed be madly fond of a cheap pleasure trip when they are content to stand in a crowded railway carriage for twelve long hours in one day. The trip may be a cheap one but we very much doubt the pleasure of it. The passengers, however, left Carlisle in good spirits and in jest of their position in the cattle trucks made excellent imitations of the bleating of sheep.

Passengers travelling from Scotland to England were warned by the railway companies to expect trouble from the English customs officers at the Border. While the Act of Union of 1707 had abolished customs between the two countries England had retained the right to tax whisky and other spirits imported from Scotland. This fact was impressed on 400 Glaswegian participants in the first ever rail excursion from

Scotland to England in July 1846 when English customs men swooped on them as they stepped from the train at Berwick and rummaged through their picnic baskets confiscating the whisky which was a standard refreshment on such occasions. Delays were experienced at the Border while trains were searched. 'Travellers who trust to the expeditions and bustle of a railway station to aid them in their contraband pursuit very much deceive themselves,' warned the *Berwick Advertiser* in reporting that six bottles of whisky had been removed from the luggage of a gentleman proceeding from Edinburgh to London. An Act of Parliament was required before the customs hazard was removed from Anglo-Scottish rail travel.

Long before the Anglo-Scottish rail links were forged Scotland had its own independent and highly individual railway system. Prestonpans, one of the battles of the Forty-Five was fought over a waggon-way. The Kilmarnock & Troon Railway, opened on 6 July 1812, was the first railway in Scotland for which an Act of Parliament was obtained. Engineered by William Jessop its purpose was to carry the Duke of Portland's coal from Kilmarnock to the harbour of Troon. Horse power was used although a Stephenson-built engine was employed briefly but unsuccessfully, its failure being due to the crude rails rather than the locomotive itself. Contemporary advertisements announced that the Kilmarnock & Troon carried passengers at a shilling for the single journey, although officially the management denied that the line was a passenger one. In answer to an inquiry from a government department the secretary explained coyly 'The Kilmarnock & Troon Railway Company have never run any passengers on their own account nor does their Act empower them to levy a duty on individual passengers. A few carriages for the conveyance of passengers travel on the line and a small tonnage is taken for each time the carriage passes estimating so many persons to constitute a ton.' To weigh people and carry them as freight was as neat a way as any of avoiding the tax then levied on railway travellers.

The Monkland & Kirkintilloch Railway was the first railway not only in Scotland but in Britain to obtain an Act to operate using locomotive power. The line was opened on 1 October 1826 to carry coal from Palacecraig pit near Airdrie to the Forth & Clyde Canal at Kirkintilloch. Horse traction was used until 1831 when two engines, the first to be built in Glasgow, were put to work. There was a hitch when the engines were found to be too big to pass through a tunnel half way along the railway. The engines worked the line on either side of the tunnel and horses took the trains through the tunnel until the roof was taken off. The Monkland & Kirkintilloch management showed that it was much in advance of its time when it placed a wagon ferry on the canal. Coal wagons coming down the rail-

BY AUTHORITY.

PUBLIC  NOTICE.

The **PUBLIC** are requested to take Notice, that the Transmission of all **FOREIGN** and **COLONIAL SPIRITS** between Scotland and England, by Land, is contrary to Law.

Spirits Distilled in Scotland can only be transmitted, by Land, in quantities exceeding Twenty Gallons, accompanied by an Excise Permit; the full rate of English Duty having been previously paid.

All Scotch Spirits found in Transit, per the Caledonian Railway, in less quantities than Twenty Gallons, and all such Spirits of that or any greater quantity unaccompanied by the necessary Permit, are liable to be seized by the Officers of the Excise.

The Caledonian Railway Company refuse to undertake the Conveyance of Spirits, except when the conditions of the Excise Regulations have been complied with, and when they are supplied with the Name and Address both of the party sending and the party to receive the Consignment.

All Packages containing Liquids of any description are liable to detention, on suspicion; to avoid which, it is desirable their contents should be stated at the time of Booking.

By order,

J. W. CODDINGTON, *Secy.*

Peter Brown, Printer, 19 St James' Square, Edinburgh.

way ran on to the ferry and were taken directly to consumers in canal-side factories or to ocean-going ships.

Hitherto railways had acted as links between sources of raw material and waterways. The year 1831 saw the opening of three Scottish railways which were not feeders to waterways but railways in their own right. These were the Garnkirk & Glasgow, the Edinburgh & Dalkeith and the Dundee & Newtyle. All were instantly successful. By the end of 1831 there was no longer any doubt that the railway was a reliable and efficient means of transport the like of which had never been seen before.

After the little railways came the trunk lines. By February 1842 Edinburgh and Glasgow were linked by a magnificently-engineered main line which, with minimum alteration, was able to cope with the 90mph Inter-city express of the 1970s. Trunk lines were built from Glasgow to Greenock and to Ayr. In 1846 the North British main line from Edinburgh to Berwick was opened. The great lateral trunk line begun by the Caledonian in 1848 was continued by a system of end-on railways—the Scottish Central, the Scottish Midland Junction and the Aberdeen Railway—to provide an unbroken route from London to Aberdeen by 1850. In the same year the Glasgow & South Western Railway began operating a through route between Glasgow, Kilmarnock, Dumfries and Carlisle. By 1858 the

railway had spread its tentacles across country from Aberdeen to Inverness and in 1863 there was opened the stupendous line that crossed the Grampians at a height of 1484 feet and gave Inverness a direct route to the south.

For 30 years the Scottish railway system developed more or less in piecemeal fashion. By 1864 upwards of a hundred companies were operating, many of them very small. In 1865–6 the pattern changed abruptly. All but a handful of the small companies merged to form five large groups mainly on a territorial basis. The railways emanating from Inverness became the Highland Railway, and those round Aberdeen and the north-east formed the Great North of Scotland Railway. The Glasgow & South Western dominated Renfrewshire, Ayrshire and Dumfriesshire. The North British, centred in Edinburgh, sought to monopolise the east, the Borders and Fife, while the Caledonian from its base in Glasgow absorbed the Scottish Central, the Scottish North Eastern and other lines to become, in its own estimation the National Line. The large new companies were the ICIs and EMIs of their day. Their boards claimed the best brains in the land. To investors railway shares were as good as gilt-edged. Railways were the growth industry of the age. By 1913 the Scottish railways had a capital value of £179,205,342. Shareholders' meetings were occasions of some importance. The following notice issued to the

Left: The east end of Waverley station Edinburgh. The prison on the hill was often mistaken for the Castle by uninformed visitors.

staff of the North British by a general manager was typical:

> Stationmasters, guards and others are reminded of the special general meeting of shareholders of the company to be held in Edinburgh on 10th January on which occasion the trains to and from Edinburgh are expected to be very heavy. The stationmasters at the terminal stations will be careful to provide those trains by which shareholders are likely to travel with ample first class carriage accommodation.

The railway changed the way of life of the whole population. What had been a treat for the few became the commonplace of the masses. A trip to the seaside, hitherto an impossible dream of the urban dweller, suddenly came within his financial scope. The Glasgow, Paisley, Kilmarnock & Ayr Railway had estimated that 21,350 passengers a year would use the line; in the first year 137,117 passenger journeys were recorded. Lethargic coastal villages blossomed into bustling holiday resorts, and a new industry was born. Upper-crust city dwellers attracted by the speed, comfort and convenience of the trains forsook their city mansions and moved out to country villas. Often the new commuters were cosseted by the railway companies who wooed them with offers of free season tickets. The Edinburgh & Glasgow Railway founded an entirely new community on barren moorland by offering potential builders of houses at Lenzie a free season ticket to Glasgow for ten years if the house cost £1000, with a year of free travel added for every £100 spent above that figure. Stone and other materials for the new towns were carried free by rail and timetables were adjusted to suit the whims of the new town dwellers. The technique was repeated as late as 1933 when the London Midland & Scottish Railway and a Glasgow builder offered free season tickets to persons purchasing houses at the developing suburb of Clarkston near Glasgow. The builder erected and furnished a showhouse in the main concourse of Glasgow Central station and visitors were given free day return tickets to Clark-

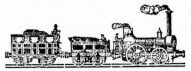

GLASGOW & AYRSHIRE RAILWAY.

GRAND PLEASURE EXCURSIONS
To AYR, KILMARNOCK, &c.

ON THURSDAY FIRST, 21st OCTOBER, Parties will be conveyed at the undernoted Moderate Rates :—

To AYR.	To KILMARNOCK.
At Half-past 7 Morning.	At Half-past 8 Morning.
Do. 10 Do.	Do. 11 Forenoon.
Do. 1 Afternoon.	Do. 2 Afternoon.

FARES.

			1st Class.	2d Class.
From GLASGOW to AYR	and BACK,	9s	...	6s
Do. MONKTON	do.	8s 3d	...	5s 8d
Do. TROON	do.	7s 6d	...	5s 3d
Do. IRVINE	do.	6s 9d	..	4s 6d
Do. KILWINNING	do.	6s	...	4s 2d
Do. STEWARTON	do.	5s 3d	...	3s 5d
Do. KILMARNOCK	do.	6s	...	4s 6d

RETURNING TO GLASGOW :

From AYR, at a Quarter-past 2 o'Clock Afternoon, and 5 o'Clock Evening.

From KILMARNOCK, at 2 o'Clock Afternoon, and at 5 o'Clock Evening.

☞ *All the Trains have three Classes of Carriages.*

NOTE.—As the above Trains do not Call at all the Intermediate Stations, particular attention is requested to the Company's Time-Bill, to be had at the Stations.

J. FAIRFUL SMITH, Secretary.

Glasgow Station, 14 Bridge-street, }
15th October, 1847. }

RACES AT BOGSIDE, IRVINE,
ON SATURDAY, 23D OCTOBER.

A TRAIN of First and Second-Class Carriages will leave GLASGOW at Half-past 10 o'Clock Forenoon, for the RACE-COURSE; when Parties will be Conveyed from GLASGOW, PAISLEY, JOHNSTONE, BEITH, KILBIRNIE, DALRY, and KILWINNING; and Return from the RACE-COURSE at Half-past 5 o'Clock Afternoon.

Horses and Carriages will be conveyed by all the Trains to and from Irvine Station, near the Race-Ground; and to prevent disappointment timely notice should be given.

GLASGOW STATION, 14 BRIDGE STREET, }
16th October, 1847. }

Above: Glasgow & Ayrshire Railway notices.

TO BUILDERS.

The DIRECTORS of the EDINBURGH and GLASGOW RAILWAY COMPANY are prepared to grant

FREE TICKETS

TO PARTIES WHO MAY

BUILD VILLAS

within a Mile of any of the Stations on the Line, not being Town Stations, on the following terms :—

Certified Cost of Villa.	Free Ticket for Years.
£500	5
600	6
700	7
800	8
900	9
1000	10

and so on, an additional year for every additional £100 in the Cost of a Villa.

 TICKETS TRANSFERABLE TO A YEARLY TENANT, IF THE HOUSE IS NOT OCCUPIED BY OWNER.

Further Information may be known on application at Company's Offices, George Square, Glasgow.

Top left: A Conner CR 2–4–0 at Perth.

Right: A Caledonian engine driver dwarfed by the 8ft 2in driving wheel of his Conner single.

Bottom left: Edinburgh & Glasgow Railway Villa tickets.

ston if they expressed a desire to view the site.

Every facet of human activity benefited from the coming of the railway. There were railway prison vans with cells in place of compartments in which convicted criminals were taken to Peterhead and other sombre resorts. There were railway hearses much used in country districts where bad or non-existent roads made conventional funerals impossible. Fathers chartered trains to take guests to their daughters' weddings. Families went on holiday in special family saloons which could be attached to ordinary trains for a modest fee. There were special carriages for invalids. Sundays saw the mass movement of theatricals. Even modest towns had thriving theatres then, and after the final curtain on Saturday nights props and personnel were rushed to the nearest station for transit to the next point on the circuit. On 13 January 1907 *Sorrows of Satan* moved from Clydebank to Newcastle, *Babes in the Wood* from Glasgow to Kirkcaldy and *The Freaks* from Glasgow to Edinburgh. Edinburgh dispatched *Spessardy's Bears* to Coventry, *Music Hall Artistes* to Liverpool and the *Crystal Gazers* to Glasgow while *Honour Thy Father* moved from Dunfermline to Glasgow.

By all accounts the theatrical specials were merry trains, but they could not have been merrier than the Sunday School excursion trains that thronged the rails on summer Saturday afternoons. On 5 June 1923, 39 such trains were on the move around Glasgow and 13 in the Edinburgh area on the London & North Eastern system alone. Between 1.45 and 2.32 that afternoon Springburn, a northern Glasgow suburb, dispatched 800 adults and 1460 children. On the same day nearly 8000 passengers, mostly children, were handled at the three stations on the Milngavie branch. According to the official notice one train conveyed 1300 passengers. Some of the journeys were surprisingly short. A

party of 150 adults and 300 children marched a mile or more from North Kelvinside United Free Church to Maryhill station for a six-minute ride to Bardowie. But the children had the great thrill of going by train—that was the thing.

The railways put sport on a new footing, for trains enabled supporters to 'follow' their favourite teams. Stations were built to service football grounds. The Caledonian built a platform beside a curling pond on their Stirling-Perth main line. Even the hunt went by train. An instruction to North British staff on 9 February 1907 read, 'The 4pm express Glasgow-Edinburgh must call at Linlithgow to lift passengers in connection with the Hunt. Care must be taken to see that straw is provided in the van for the conveyance of the hounds'. Golf was a major beneficiary. The first railway in the East Neuk of Fife cut across the famous links of St Andrews. The Ayrshire line passed Barassie, Troon and Prestwick in quick succession. The railways created courses which became internationally

(PRIVATE.)

EDINBURGH AND NORTHERN RAILWAY.

CIRCULAR TO STATION AGENTS.

THE remark has frequently been made to me that there is a slowness and want of energy at many of the Stations, manifested in the passengers being allowed to stand on the platforms, the servants not showing activity in discovering the class of carriages into which the passengers are to go, and pointing them to their seats—in the carriage doors not being speedily opened to allow passengers to get quickly out—in the luggage not being placed on the train with dispatch—and in the Starting-Bell (which sometimes has to be searched for) not being timeously rung, and the signal to start promptly given. To a certain extent these causes of delay have been removed, but at various Stations they subsist still to a great degree; and as it is a subject of remark, the Station Agents will perceive that it is due to the Company, as well as to themselves, that occasion for such remark should cease. A section of the public will always be complainers, but a larger section are familiar with railway travelling on old and well-organised railways, and readily detect and mark any deficiency in the order and energy of the officers. Moreover, in every train there are travellers of that class, and it is well that that fact should exercise a constant impression on the Officers of this Company.

One minute occupied longer at a Station than is necessary, results, if repeated at each Station, in occasioning a delay of seventeen minutes on the journey between Edinburgh and Perth. And although one minute may appear an insignificant delay at any one Station, the Station Agents will perceive how serious the result becomes, when the number of Stations is considered, with the limited time allowed for making the journey.

I have marked delays arise thus—The Starting-Bell is not rung by the Porter because he sees the Engineman is taking in water or is oiling the engine, and therefore waits till the Engineman appears to be quite ready; or the Guard is occupying himself, after the passengers and luggage have been attended to, and he, too, is waited upon; hence arise confusion and delay. The Bell ought to be rung instantly after the passengers and luggage have been attended to, the Guard being thereby made aware that *his* signal to start should be given, and the Engineman that *he* must be prepared for the signal.

Let all the Station Agents, therefore, be careful to remove any ground of complaint of want of dispatch and energy at their several Stations, that the Trains may be detained the least possible time consistently with the comfort of the passengers.

In the collection of the Tickets at certain of the Stations great delay has been permitted, for which the Station Agents have been to blame, inasmuch as the repeated instructions given, as to the method of collecting them, were not attended to as they ought to have been. Exertions, it is hoped, will be made to have this duty more efficiently performed.

Should unnecessary delays be occasioned by the Guards or Enginemen, it is the imperative duty of the Station Agents to report such without delay.

It is proper that each Station should be supplied with all useful information with regard to the starting of the various Railways and Coaches, particularly those connected with this Line. That bills giving such information should be posted and hung up with some degree of order, and where they can be consulted by Passengers. At one of the Stations, recently, it was pointed out to the Station Agent that his sheet of Bradshaw was more than a month old, and yet he had not made known at the Head Office that the last-issued sheet had not reached him.

As the evenings are now getting soon dark, the Station Agents will be careful to see that the Signal Lights are in good order. Before dark, they should also satisfy themselves that the Carriages and Waggons are standing properly on the Sidings, and that the Choke Blocks are closed and locked.

The Station Agents are invited to make any suggestions, from time to time, which appear likely to forward the interests of the Company.

HENRY LEES.

COMPANY'S OFFICES, }
EDINBURGH, 1st September, 1848. }

Circular to station agents, Edinburgh & Northern Rly 1848.

renowned, and Gleneagles and Turnberry are names that spring to mind. Large, ornate hotels were built to accommodate the golfers. When the Glasgow & South Western Railway built a hotel overlooking its own golf course and the sea at Turnberry the main entrance was put at the back of the building facing the railway. James Miller the architect explained, 'I would point out that the principal traffic using the hotel will be by the station entrance and not by the west front while any driving that would take place from the west front would usually be in fine weather when such a cover (a porch had been suggested) would be unnecessary.' Turnberry hotel still overlooks the golf course and the sea, but its main entrance now faces west and a gorse-choked ditch at the back of the building is all that remains of the railway.

Any Scottish town or village shop that sold local view postcards knew that the subject next in favour to the High Street was the railway station. Stations were friendly places and local folks were proud of them. Large or small Scottish stations were full of character, and some still are. To southern eyes the typical Scottish station had cottage type buildings flanked by pines or flowers in tubs set against a backdrop of mountains. Yet the biggest stations outside London were not in the English provinces but in Scotland. Edinburgh Waverley with its 21 platforms was second only to Waterloo in size. Glasgow Central at its peak handled 22,000,000 passengers a year. Even today the Central has a greater number of daily train movements than any station in Britain. At rush hours trains are double-banked and even triple-banked at its platforms.

Great as were the blessings brought to individuals by the railway, they were as nothing compared with the vast changes wrought in the Scottish economy. With the coming of the railway the industrial revolution took a vast leap forward. Both Edinburgh and Glasgow had suffered recurring coal famines due to frost and storms making roads and canals impassable, and factories and homes had been deprived of fuel for long periods. The new railways were impervious to the weather. Lines spread to every pit and coal rolled regularly and with ease to wherever it was needed. Prices plummeted. Existing factories expanded and new establishments sprang up along the railway. Iron was replacing timber for shipbuilding on the Clyde and the railway was the ideal medium for transporting heavy iron plates from the mills of Lanarkshire. Ports favoured with rail connections soon attained a prosperity undreamed of in the pre-railway age. Troon and Ardrossan in Ayrshire and Grangemouth, Bo'ness and Methil in the east were examples.

The geography of Scotland presented a mighty challenge to civil and mechanical engineers alike. There were mountain passes to be conquered and great firths to be spanned. Joseph Mitchell built the 103 miles of the Highland Railway main line from Forres to Dunkeld, crossing two mountain barriers at heights well above 1000ft in the process, in the incredible time of 23 months. (The much vaunted 'mountain' section of the Lancaster & Carlisle Railway, half the length and with a summit less than 1000ft, took over two years to complete.) The North British, faced with a sea estuary two miles wide built the longest bridge in the world, and when it fell down built another one. The Forth Bridge was the first of the great steel railway bridges, and on the Mallaig Extension of the West Highland Railway the extensive use of mass concrete for bridge construction was unique at the time. The mechanical engineers had to produce locomotives capable of surmounting the gradients created by their civil brethren. That was no problem in the land of James Watt and Henry Bell. Within a decade of the opening of the Garnkirk & Glasgow Railway the city of Glasgow was exporting locomotives to world markets. It was no accident that some of the most powerful engines within the United Kingdom ran on Scottish rails.

By the time of the consolidation of 1865 railwaymen had come to be regarded as something special. Unlike factory workers and shipbuilders, railwaymen worked for the most part in full view of the public. Regular travellers got to know them. There was a sense of awe about the driver leaning from the cab of his engine at the departure of a great express. The signalman darting along his frame amid the clashing of levers could be seen by all through the windows of his workplace. Railwaymen were incredibly loyal to their own companies. To the Caledonian man there was no line like the Caley, an attitude that was handed down from generation to generation. A good Caledonian man would have viewed with trepidation the prospect of having a

North British son-in-law. And so it was with all the companies.

The companies fought each other with ferocity and ruthlessness. Hundreds of thousands of pounds were spent in legal fees in attempts to keep rivals out of territory companies considered to be theirs. Rival, almost parallel lines were built to towns where the traffic hardly justified one line. Rarely was there a protest from the shareholders. The rich rewards reaped elsewhere, and especially in the mineral fields, masked the losses resulting from extravagant construction. Nowhere was railway rivalry fiercer than on the lines leading from Glasgow to the Clyde coast. The Caledonian, North British and Glasgow & South Western dispatched trains from Glasgow to their respective coast termini within minutes of each other and continued the contest on water with their own steamers in an all-out effort to capture the resort traffic. A bizarre manifestation of railway rivalry was the racing of 1888 and 1895. In 1888 the East Coast group of companies (the Great Northern, the North Eastern and the North British) raced the West Coast group (London & North Western and Caledonian) from London to Edinburgh. In 1895 the racecourse extended from London all the way to Aberdeen, with the trains being handed over like batons in a mad country-long relay race at company boundaries. For a month the rival trains ran faster and faster paying no attention to timetables or public convenience. Modern research has shown that the episode was utterly futile and foolhardy and, on the twisting Scottish lines where severe speed restrictions imposed for the public protection were ignored, criminally dangerous. The railway managements, in the end thoroughly frightened, abandoned the races, never again to resume them. Henceforward they sought to attract traffic by offering comfort rather than speed. The Caledonian, for instance, produced its famous Grampian twelve-wheeled coaches for its Aberdeen service—arguably the most luxurious passenger vehicles ever seen in daily use in Britain—and forced the North British to depart from its lamentable standard in passenger stock.

The old companies tended to be paternal towards their staffs. Managements joined in their social life as at the grand soirées where music, uplift and good food (but not drink) were the ingredients. Who nowadays would go to a company-sponsored concert where the musical items were interspersed with *three* sermons by local ministers? Every year the directors of the Great North of Scotland Railway invited selected staff to a reception and banquet. A ticket for 'the directors' reception' had the prestige of an illuminated address. Mammoth staff excursions were the feature of the age. The Highland and Great North of Scotland railways were not the best of friends but on one day of the year they co-operated to the extent that the GNS staff excursion from Aberdeen to Inverness was able to pass on a recipriocal course the HR staff excursion from Inverness to Aberdeen. When the Caledonian took 14,000 employees and friends from Glasgow to Carlisle in 14 trains in 1899 the Prime Minister himself (Lord Rosebery) was the chief excursionist and the Lord Advocate and the Speaker of the House of Commons were among the guests.

The paternalism of some companies was overpowering. A booking clerk on the North British was sacked when his fellow citizens elected him to a local council as a representative of a political party that did not find favour in the boardroom. Six North British men who founded a co-operative trading society were likewise sacked. All the men got their jobs back following public and parliamentary pressure. In time the pro-

Left: A Caledonian stationmaster.

Above: A Skye bogie of the Highland Railway on a local passenger train in LMS days.

scribed co-operative became a very large trading organisation which used for its official seal an impression of a North British locomotive.

Alexander Robb, a clerk at Cruden Bay on the GNS, was disappointed not to be invited to the 1898 directors' reception. He duly presented himself at the Aberdeen Music Hall ticketless and drunk and proceeded to conduct himself in a discreditable manner in front of the hierarchy. In the following week a contrite Robb stood before the superintendent pledging himself 'to become an abstainer and conduct himself in such a manner as to give no cause whatever for complaint' His name was duly inscribed in the Offence Book alongside those of his numerous colleagues who had blotted their copybooks over the years. There was, for instance, A. Wilkie, goods guard, who mishandled a shunt movement at Cullen one day and whose crime was 'allowing his train to run from Cullen to Portknockie with vehicles on both sides of his engine.' John Peterham, porter, Schoolhill 'snipped return half of ticket in error' and won himself a caution, as did Alexander Pirrie, booking clerk at Banff Bridge, 'for booking passengers to Dyce on trains that did not stop.' N. Fletcher, booking clerk Cullen, was cautioned

'for running short of tickets', while a severe caution was administered to the porter at Kemnay who took a passenger to Kintore for a joyride on the branch engine. G. Clark, Ladybridge, was cautioned 'for giving impertinence on the telegraph,' as was William Leslie, signalman, Kinaldie, 'who wrote offensive remarks on invoices'. William Milne was severely cautioned after an inspector found 'bills tacked on walls of waiting room and on blackboard instead of being gummed.' Percy Masson's misdemeanour had a trace of originality about it. He failed to pay his landlady for eleven weeks telling her that he received no pay from the GNS. He got the sack.

One GNS function which the participants attended with reluctance was the periodic examination for junior male clerical staff and girl clerks. The examinees, from offices and stations throughout the system, assembled at Aberdeen Joint Station ambulance hall. There were 17 candidates at the examination held on 27 April 1923, barely four months after the GNS had been absorbed by the LNER. The examiner's report survives. It is a revealing document which must be of interest to educationalists as well as to railway historians. Here are some of its conclusions.

'*Intelligence.* Percentage mark 29.4. Such a result at the age of these candidates is very disappointing. It is clear that their range of reading is limited, even of the daily press. *Arithmetic.* Five candidates received no marks at all. *Analysis.* The percentage was only 48. The subject has been mostly forgotten if ever it had been learned. Only one gets full marks and four no marks at all. In three of these four cases no marks were got for intelligence either. *Geography.* The knowledge of the map of Scotland is deplorable. One would hardly credit that 17 young people of this age could place on a blank map but an average of six places out of 20 not chosen because of their difficulty. No 3 only served to show the poverty of ideas as to what things contribute to the importance of the LNER'. However, the candidates shone at shorthand. 'The matter was distinctly difficult,' reported the examiner, 'but the candidates overcame all obstacles with the greatest of ease'.

When Prince Albert made a gift of Balmoral Castle to Queen Victoria he unwittingly added a dash of romance to Scottish railway history. The nearest station to Balmoral was Ballater, the terminus of the Deeside line, $42\frac{1}{2}$ miles west of Aberdeen. Over the years the railways were to play host to a grand pageant of Ballater-bound royal trains. Queen Victoria on her regular journeys from Osborne on the Isle of Wight to Balmoral travelled by train from Gosport to Ballater, a distance of $625\frac{1}{4}$ miles. Another royal run was Windsor to Ballater, 589 miles. There were frequent journeys by lesser members of the royal household and by foreign crowned heads.

The passage of royalty was accompanied by much pomp and ritual. Before every royal journey secret instructions were sent to senior railway staff detailing the measures required to ensure the smooth and safe passage of the royal travellers. Normally all traffic was stopped on the royal route for half an hour before the royal train was due. Goods trains on adjacent lines were shunted into sidings. Passenger trains proceeding in the opposite direction were allowed to pass the royal train although at reduced speed. Level crossing gates were padlocked and facing points were clipped and chocked with wooden keys which normally held bullhead rail tight in the chairs. A policeman was posted on every bridge. A pilot engine was sent out to run over the route 20min ahead of the royal train. The royal train itself conveyed not only the royals but the directors and senior officers of the railway involved and staff and equipment to deal with every type of emergency.

An extraordinary royal journey took place on 22 September 1896 when Their Imperial Majesties the Czar and Czarina of Russia travelled from Leith to Ballater. News of the impending journey caused a flurry in court and railway circles. The Imperial Train was timed to reach its destination in the dusk of an autumn evening, and Queen Victoria, well aware that Ballater station was fitfully lit by oil lamps, was anxious that something be done to improve the lighting. Sir Arthur Biggs wrote to Lord Kintore, 'I have today heard from the Duke of Connaught pointing out how essential it will be to have the station light enough for the Imperial Guests to recognise all including the Prince of Wales who will be waiting to receive them.' (It would not have done for the Czar of all the Russias to have stepped from the train and shaken hands with the porter.) The equerry added, 'We hope also that the station will be decorated but this is rather a delicate subject to hint even to the railway company.' In the event an electrical contractor in Aberdeen offered to provide electric lighting free 'for the advertisement' and Sir Allan MacKenzie undertook to supply 'unlimited quantities of heather and bracken.'

The Imperial Train left Junction Road (Leith) at 2.30pm and for the first $95\frac{1}{2}$ miles to Kinnaber Junction was handled by the North British. During the 2hr 14min it occupied NB metals 12 passenger trains were cancelled, 19 were shunted or diverted and 22 goods trains were retimed. For 45min before the arrival of the Imperial Train, Haymarket and St Margarets sheds were closed and no locomotive movements took place between these depots and Waverley station.

On the return journey from Ballater to Portsmouth, men were posted at intervals of not more than half a mile over the entire 624 mile route, so that every foot of track was under surveillance. Stationmasters were warned not to divulge details of the train's timings to the press.

World War I left the Scottish lines debilitated and with a question mark over their future. A proposal to combine all the Scottish lines into one large indigenous system was bitterly opposed by commercial interests, and when the expected reorganisation of the nation's railway system took place in 1923 the Scottish lines found themselves grouped with London-based companies,

Timetable planned for the journey of the Czar from Leith to Ballater on 21 September 1896. In the event the journey took place a day later.

TIME TABLE

FOR REGULATING THE PROGRESS OF

"THE IMPERIAL TRAIN,"

From JUNCTION ROAD to ABERDEEN,

En Route TO BALLATER (FOR BALMORAL)

On MONDAY, 21st SEPTEMBER 1896.

Distance from Junction Road.	STATIONS.	Arrive.	Pass.	Depart.
MILES.		P.M.	P.M.	P.M.
—	Junction Road . .	...	...	2 30
3/8	Bonnington . . .	...	2 32	..
3/4	Powderhall . .	...	2 33	...
1 1/4	Leith Walk . .	...	2 34	...
1 3/4	Easter Road . .	...	2 35	...
2	Abbeyhill . . .	...	2 37	...
3	Edinburgh (Main Down Platform) .	...	2 40	...
4 1/4	Haymarket . . .	...	2 43	...
6 1/2	Corstorphine Junction .	...	2 46	...
12 1/2	Dalmeny . . .	..	2 53	...
14 1/4	North Queensferry } Forth Bridge North }	...	2 57	...
16 1/4	Inverkeithing . .	...	3 0	...
20 3/8	Aberdour . . .	...	3 5	
23 1/8	Burntisland . . .	...	3 8	...
25 3/4	Kinghorn . .	...	3 11	...
28 7/8	Kirkcaldy . . .	...	3 14	...
30 1/4	Sinclairtown . .	...	3 16	...
31	Dysart . . .	...	3 17	...
33 3/4	Thornton Junction .	...	3 20	...
36 1/4	Markinch Junction .	...	3 23	...
39 1/8	Falkland Road . .	...	3 26	..
41 1/4	Kingskettle . .	...	3 28	...
42 1/8	Ladybank Junction .	...	3 29	..
45 3/8	Springfield . .	...	3 32	...
47 5/8	Cupar . . .	...	3 35	...
50 5/8	Dairsie . . .	...	3 38	...
53 7/8	Leuchars Junction .	...	3 41	...
57 5/8	St Fort . . .	...	3 44	...
59 5/8	Tay Bridge (South) .	...	3 46	
61 1/2	Tay Bridge (North) } Esplanade Station }	...	3 51	...
62 1/4	*Dundee (Tay Bridge Station) .	3 53	...	3 56
63	Camperdown Junction .	...	3 58	...
65 3/4	West Ferry . .	...	4 2	...
66 1/4	Broughty Ferry . .	...	4 3	...
68 3/8	Monifieth . . .	...	4 6	...
71 1/2	Barry . . .	...	4 9	...
73 1/8	Carnoustie . .	...	4 11	
74 3/8	Easthaven . . .	...	4 13	...
77 3/8	Elliot Junction . .	...	4 17	...
79 1/4	Arbroath . .	...	4 19	
79 7/8	St Vigeans Junction .	...	4 21	
82 1/4	Letham Grange . .	...	4 24	...
84 1/2	Cauldcots . .	...	4 27	...
85 1/2	Inverkeilor . .	...	4 29	
88 1/8	Lunan Bay . .	...	4 33	...
93	Montrose . .	...	4 40	...
95	Hillside . .	...	4 43	...
95 1/2	Kinnaber Junction .	...	4 44	
97 3/8	Craigo . .	...	4 47	.
99 3/4	Marykirk . . .	...	4 51	...
103	Laurencekirk . .	...	4 55	...
106 1/4	Fordoun . .	...	4 59	...
110 1/4	Drumlithie . .	...	5 3	...
112	Newmill . .	...	5 5	...
117 3/8	Stonehaven . .	...	5 11	...
122	Muchalls . .	...	5 16	
123 1/8	Newtonhill . .	...	5 18	...
125 3/8	Portlethen . .	...	5 21	...
128 3/4	Cove . .	...	5 25	...
133	Aberdeen . . } Ferryhill Junction }	5 31	...	5 50
175 5/8	Ballater . . .	7 0	...	...

* Engines to be changed.

EDINBURGH, *16th September* 1896.   (3-M)

J. CONACHER,
GENERAL MANAGER.

THE CALL OF THE GREAT NORTH.

the Caledonian, the G & SW and the Highland going to the LMS and the North British and the GNS forming the Scottish end of the LNER.

Scotland was badly hit by the post war depression. Traffic fell away as shipyards and factories closed and pits went on short time. Yet the local Scottish managements, which retained a reasonable degree of autonomy, put a brave face on the situation. There wasn't much money about, but the railways went out to get their share. These were the years of long distance excursions at rock-bottom prices. Trippers could travel from Glasgow to Aberdeen and back for 8s and to the English Lakes or Fort William for 7s. It was the era of the 'evening breather' when travellers took to the rails in thousands after tea and travelled remarkable distances at negligible cost. Aberdonians could have an evening in Elgin or Dundee for half a crown, and for the same amount citizens of Edinburgh were transported to the Clyde coast. Trains ran in duplicate and triplicate especially in fine weather when hundreds flocked from offices and factories to the stations. The railways whetted the appetites of their patrons by advertising unfamiliar routes

and destinations, some on 'foreign' teritory. A favourite was Lanark on the LMS to Portobello on the LNER. Drivers as well as passengers found themselves treading strange ground. There was one evening when the LNER ran a through excursion from Grangemouth on the Forth to Balloch on Loch Lomond. The route was via Maryhill and thence to Dumbarton and then by the Dumbarton & Balloch Joint line (LNER and LMS) to Balloch. It was a Sunday and all the Glasgow-Balloch traffic was going by the LMS route to Dumbarton, the LNER route carrying only the Helensburgh trains. When the return excursion passed Dalreoch the driver should have sounded a whistle code indicating that he was booked for the LNER route at Dumbarton East Junction, but he failed to do so. He had gone several miles before he discovered that he had taken the wrong turning and was on LMS metals.

These were the days, too, of keen competition between the LMS and the LNER for the Anglo-Scottish traffic, days when the *Royal Scot* and *Flying Scotsman* became more than ever household words. How far the companies had departed from the racing days of old was seen by the fact that they each gave their trains an agreed, but leisurely and unrealistic, 8¼ hours for their journeys. It was not until 1937 and the introduction of the LMS *Coronation Scot* and the LNER *Coronation* that the speed element, albeit carefully regulated, returned to the Anglo-Scottish rail scene.

To the Glasgow schoolboy of the 1930s there was no more thrilling outing than a tram trip to Milngavie, for there near the end of the line was something straight from the more extravagant pages of his own comics—the George Bennie Railplane. A long silver bullet, with air screws at both ends, hung from an overhead railway built above a siding from the Milngavie branch. In exchange for a sixpence the young visitor could climb the steps to the futuristic elevated station and seat himself in an armchair in the opulent saloon of the railplane. To the whirr of propellors the magic vehicle moved off smoothly over the fields.

George Bennie was a Glasgow engineer-inventor with more than a touch of eccentricity in his make up. He spent £150,000 of his own money on his railplane which he was convinced was the transport vehicle of the future. In the lavish brochure he distributed at the opening of the experimental track at Milngavie on 8 June 1930 Bennie explained, 'The George Bennie Railplane System of Transport has been originated and developed to a practical conclusion and will be a universal means of transport by land by virtue of the following factors: 1 The insistent demand for safe and rapid transport. 2 A new method of transport is urgently required in industrial centres due to the present congestion of roads. 3 A cheap method of transport is urgently required for the development of rural districts, for the transport of mails and perishable goods and for the opening up of new and underdeveloped countries.'

Bennie's brochure had an uncanny ring of the 1970s about it. 'Our railways are a national asset,' he pointed out. 'They cannot be allowed to go under in the transport competition. It is intended that the George Bennie Railplane System will restore them to their lost economic position'. Bennie saw passengers, mail and perishable freight passing overhead leaving the lines below clear for minerals and non-urgent goods. He visualised speeds of 120mph for his railplane. A mile of Bennie railway was estimated to cost £19,000 compared with £45,000 for a mile of standard double line track.

The GBR attracted wide publicity and several serious inquiries which Bennie pursued vigorously. He produced a scheme for a railplane system above the LNER Edinburgh-Glasgow main line. For a time there were hopes that the 500-mile railway between Djibouti and Addis Ababa (on which waterless desert made operation by steam locomotives difficult) would switch to the Bennie system. The Abyssinian war put paid to that. There was a scheme for taking a Bennie line across Morecambe Bay and another for a seafront line to replace the trams between Blackpool and St Annes. All Bennie's efforts were brought to nought by the outbreak of World War II.

During the war Bennie worked steadily on improving his invention and he was geared to exploit his system in the productive years which he felt would follow the end of the war. On 28 September 1946 there was incorporated in Edinburgh the George Bennie Airspeed Railway Ltd, a company with the object of taking over from Bennie the world rights of his system together with all the letters patent and all the drawings, models and benefits from current contracts and negotiations. Bennie owned 19,999 of the 20,000 shares and he was to be paid £150,000 in cash (that being the sum he had spent on the system) plus £5,000,000 in instalments from world-wide profits accruing from his system.

The story of the George Bennie Airspeed Railway is told in a sad file of company documents now reposing in the Scottish Record Office. Every year as required by law the company submitted a report on the appropriate form to the Registrar of Companies. In all of these reports Bennie gave as his 'usual residential address' the Central Hotel, Glasgow, a far from cheap establishment. Successive reports were endorsed 'no trading has taken place.' When no return was received at the Company Registration Office for 1955 a letter was sent to the registered office of the company in Glasgow indicating that if the requisite information was not forthcoming within three months the company would be deleted from the register. The letter was returned marked 'gone away'. A second letter produced similar results. The company secretary when approached stated that he had resigned in 1953 and knew nothing of Bennie although he believed he had undergone an operation in a London hospital. The manager of the Central Hotel explained that Mr Bennie had not resided in the hotel for some time and had left no forwarding address. In fact, George Bennie was dead. The George

Above: Glasgow Central in the electrified seventies; two of the new BR Class 87 electric locomotives wait to leave with early evening expresses to the south on 23 May 1974, on the left 87011 with the 18.05 to Manchester and on the right 87003 with the 17.30 to London.

Bennie Airspeed Railway Ltd was listed as dissolved in the *Edinburgh Gazette* of 27 November 1956. The abandoned railplane, dull red all over, mouldered away in the field at Milngavie until the 1960s when it was sold for scrap.

In 1946 the railways made a brave attempt to take up where they had left off in 1939. The favourite excursions of old were resumed and for a time the patrons of the past took gleefully to the rail. In that first peacetime summer for seven years the resorts were crowded, the railway-owned steamers on the Clyde and Loch Lomond doing particularly well. But the new era of sunshine, packed trains and crowded decks was to be short-lived. As after World War I change was in the air and it came with nationalisation in 1948. With the ending of petrol rationing, railway passengers in growing numbers took to the roads in the newly acquired family car. Travel patterns changed drastically. The branch lines were the first to suffer and soon came those ominous Saturdays when trains ran for the last time on a clutch of branches. Then it was the turn of the main lines, although it had to be conceded that some of the closures at least

were due to the unnecessary duplication of routes by rival companies in the days of unbridled competition.

In spite of the surgery of the recent past Scotland's railways still retain their atmosphere and fascination. All the great scenic lines of the Highlands and West Highlands, with the exception of the Dunblane-Crianlarich section of the Callander & Oban Railway, remain intact. The longest passenger trains on British Rail today are to be seen among the mountains of the Highlands, the afternoon southbound train out of Inverness on a summer Sunday normally being loaded to 16 vehicles. Double track over the Grampians, precipitately removed in the dark Beeching days, is now being restored to cope with *increasing* traffic. Electrification has revitalised the suburban services round Glasgow. Main line electrics glide from Glasgow to London in five hours and there is a train every two hours most of the day and on peak days hourly. Scotland's lines have much to offer. It is hoped that this backward look into the colourful past will help the modern traveller to savour al' the better what he finds in Scotland today.

2 THE OBAN LINE

Above: The first of the class, No 191, as LMS No 14619, tackling a bank between Dalmally and Tyndrum with a typical train of the 1920s.

The railways which serve the Highlands and West Highlands have a special fascination for travellers. The sight of locomotives battling with heavy gradients is exciting. The last engines specifically designed to deal with the problems of the Oban line were William Pickersgill's 191 class 4–6–0s built by the North British Locomotive Co in 1922.

Below: The 191 class were small, neat engines. In this picture a low lens angle lends one of the class a majestic appearance as it coasts down a gentle gradient near Dalmally.

Above: Callander station, east end.

Top left: Callander station, west end, with a Caledonian Drummond Jumbo in blue livery performing a shunt move. Note the clock on the overbridge.

Bottom left: The forerunner of the 191 class on the line was McIntosh's 4–6–0 of 1903. No 55, first of the class, is seen leaving Callander with a westbound train.

Left: A 55 class 4–6–0, assisted by a Jumbo, with both engines in blue livery, leave Oban with a Glasgow train.

Bottom left: A Caledonian non-gangwayed brake composite carriage seen here in LMS livery. This type of coach had toilet facilities with access by internal corridors but it was not possible for passengers to walk through to other coaches. It was a very useful type of vehicle on longer runs by stopping trains where there were no dining cars, and was also used by the Caledonian and LMS on certain branch services.

Below: No 439 was the first of a class of 0–4–4 tank designed by J F McIntosh for branch and suburban work and first introduced in 1900. In this evocative study of a branch line train No 439 is seen at Killin Junction.

3 DRUIMUACHDAR PASS

The great Inverness engineer Joseph Mitchell built the 103-mile main line of the Highland Railway (then the Inverness & Perth Junction) from Forres to Dunkeld in 23 months, a staggering feat remembering that he had to conquer one summit, Dava, 1052ft above sea level and another, Druimuachdar Pass in the Grampians, 1484ft above sea level. Druimuachdar Pass, the highest point ever reached by a British main line, dominated life on the Highland. Day and night, year in, year out, the railway wrestled with the problem of getting its trains over the Pass, often in the worst possible weather conditions.

Left: The summit.

Right: No 149 *Duncraig Castle* nears the summit with an express.

The Highland Railway was always in search of increased power as the trains handed over by the southern companies at Perth became heavier. Christopher Cumming's Clan 4–6–0 was a logical successor to the Castle. *Clan Cameron*, No 57, is seen, *below*, among the mountains. *Clan Mackinnon* required the assistance of *Ben Clebaig* with a long summer tourist train, *below right*.

The unending search for power extended to goods engines and led to the introduction on the Highland of the first British 4–6–0 in 1894. *Above:* Jones Goods No 109 approaches the summit. *Below:* No 81, a representative of the next generation of goods engine, the Cumming Clan Goods, is seen hard at work with a cattle train.

4
A HIGHLAND
BRANCH

Right: No 102 had expected to be working in South America in 1892 but instead found itself jogging up and down a Highland branch. Dübs & Co of Glasgow were left with this engine and her sister on their hands when the Uruguay Eastern Railway fell on hard times and the Highland Railway bought them. They proved so successful that the company ordered three more of the class within a year. No 102 is seen here at Aberfeldy as she looked after Peter Drummond had given her his standard chimney and boiler mountings.

Above: Aberfeldy station.

Right: First class on the branch.

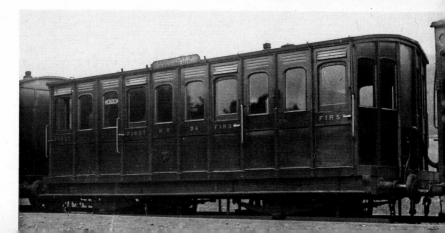

5 WHEN ROYALTY TRAVELLED

Above: When not on royal duties No 123 performed menial tasks. The engine is seen here on a local train south of Aberdeen.

Above right: A Caledonian official takes a last look at the engines before they take over the royal train. The two Dunalastair IIs will head the train and No 123 will set off 20 minutes ahead to ensure that all is well on the line and give warning of the royal train's approach. No 123 was royal train pilot for many years. No 123 is painted in the orthodox, darkish St Rollox blue while the Dunalastairs display the lighter Perth blue. It is said that the master painter at Perth works added Chinese white to the official paint.

Right: Instructions for the operation of the royal train from Leith to Ballater for the Czar of Russia on 22 September 1896, including train alterations, on the Dundee & Arbroath Joint Railway.

AMENDED NOTICE.

DUNDEE AND ARBROATH JOINT RAILWAY.

MANAGER'S OFFICE,
DUNDEE, *September 19th,* 1896.

JOURNEY OF HIS IMPERIAL MAJESTY, THE CZAR OF RUSSIA,

FROM JUNCTION ROAD (LEITH) TO ABERDEEN,

Via Forth and Tay Bridges, Arbroath, and Lunan Bay,

En Route TO BALLATER,

On **TUESDAY,** the 22nd **SEPTEMBER 1896.**

Instructions for Working the Imperial Train and the Pilot Engine which is to precede it over the Dundee and Arbroath Joint Line.

1.—A Pilot Engine will leave Dundee (Tay Bridge Station) at 3.36 P.M. (20 minutes **before** the Imperial Train), pass Camperdown Junction at 3.38 P.M., and St Vigeans Junction at 4.1 P.M. The Driver must run at the speed indicated by the accompanying Time Table, in order that he may occupy the same time from Station to Station as the Imperial Train, and uniformly maintain the interval of 20 minutes throughout the journey.

2.—The Imperial Train will leave Junction Road (Leith) at 2.30 P.M., and Dundee (Tay Bridge) at 3.56 P.M., for Aberdeen, and will depart from, pass, and arrive at the various Stations according to the accompanying Time Table.

3.—Drivers of the Imperial Train are reminded of the instructions now in force as to the restriction of speed when passing over certain portions of the Dundee and Arbroath Joint Line, with which they must strictly comply. They must also reduce speed when passing over the Line between Arbroath (South Box) and St Vigeans Junction to 10 miles an hour.

4.—Competent Telegraph Men, under the charge of North British Company's Telegraph Superintendent, will accompany the Train with the necessary Instrument and Appliances by which communication can be at once established at any place in case of need. In that event the "Call Signal" for the Imperial Train will be "I. T.," and messages sent from the Imperial Train will be Prefixed "R. L.," and take precedence of all other messages except those bearing the Prefix "S. R. M." or "D. G."

5.—No Train, Engine, or Vehicle whatever must enter upon or cross the Down Main Line at any point on the Joint Line, for at least 30 minutes before the time named in the accompanying Time Table for the passing of the Imperial Train, except the Pilot which precedes the Imperial Train at an interval of 20 minutes. All Shunting Operations on the Lines adjoining the Main Line must be suspended for the same period.

6.—Should any of the Down Trains be out of time, they must be shunted into Sidings at such Stations as will ensure their being at a stand 30 minutes before the Imperial Train is due to pass them.

7.—No Trains or Light Engines, except Passenger Trains, must be allowed to travel between any two Stations on the Up Line from the time the Pilot is due to pass until the Imperial Train has passed between those Stations on the Down Line; and as regards Passenger Trains on the Up Line, they must be slowed to a speed not exceeding ten miles an hour while the Imperial Train is passing them on the Down Line; Drivers must also avoid whistling.

DUNDEE AND ARBROATH JOINT RAILWAY.

MEMORANDUM OF TRAINS to be Shunted into Sidings, or otherwise dealt with, on the Afternoon of **Tuesday, 22nd September 1896,** to ensure **Safety,** and (as far as possible) **Absence of Noise** on the passing **Down** of the **IMPERIAL TRAIN.**

DOWN.

3.15 p.m. Joint Passenger Train, Dundee East to Arbroath, must be started and worked punctually to Table Time **to Barry, where it must shunt and remain until the Imperial Train has passed.**

Note.—It will thereafter precede, as quickly as possible, *to Arbroath, the 3.50 p.m. Train, Dundee Tay Bridge to Aberdeen, and call at Easthaven and Elliot Junction, in lieu of the 3.30 p.m. ex Tay Bridge.*

3.30 p.m. N.B. Passenger Train, Dundee Tay Bridge to Arbroath, **must not start** until the Imperial Train has passed.

Note.—If this Train is running ahead of the 3.50 p.m. ex Tay Bridge, or 4.0 p.m. ex Dundee East, and overtaken by them, it must be shunted where necessary to allow them to pass.

3.40 p.m. Joint Passenger Train, Dundee East to Broughty Ferry, **will not be run.** *Engine, Vehicles, and Guard to work 4.25 p.m. ex Broughty Ferry. Must leave Dundee East at 3.20 p.m. prompt.*

3.40 p.m. North British Goods Train, Arbroath to Forfar, **must leave Arbroath at 3.35 p.m.,** or sooner if possible.

3.50 p.m. North British Passenger Train, Dundee Tay Bridge to Aberdeen, **must not start** until the Imperial Train has passed.

4.0 p.m. Caledonian Passenger Train, Dundee East to Montrose, and 4.5 p.m. and 4.10 p.m. Caledonian Trains, Dundee East to Kirriemuir, **must not start from Dundee East** until the Imperial Train has passed (if late).

4.10 p.m. North British Passenger Train, Dundee Tay Bridge to Aberdeen, **must not start** until the Imperial Train has passed (if late).

4.15 p.m. Caledonian Passenger Train, Arbroath to Guthrie, **must not start** until the Imperial Train has passed.

UP.

2.15 p.m. Caledonian Train, Montrose to Dundee East, **must remain at West Ferry** until the Imperial Train has passed Camperdown Junction. *The 2.15 p.m. must be slowed to a speed of not exceeding ten miles an hour while the Imperial Train is passing it on the Down Line.*

2.40 p.m. N.B. Goods Train, Forfar to Arbroath, must be worked so as to arrive at Arbroath **as much before 3.30 p.m. as possible.**

2.52 p.m. North British Goods Train, St Vigeans Junction to Dundee, Tay Bridge, **must shunt and remain at Easthaven** until the Imperial Train has passed.

3.0 p.m. Caledonian Passenger Train, Forfar to Arbroath, **must be worked punctually to Arbroath.**

3.0 p.m. N.B. Goods Train, Montrose to Arbroath, **must not leave Montrose** until the Imperial Train has passed.

3.17 p.m. Light Engine, Broughty Ferry to Dundee East, **must leave at 3.5 p.m.,** and arrive at Dundee East at 3.17 p.m.

3.20 p.m. N.B. Cattle Train, Montrose to Dundee, **must not leave Montrose** until the Imperial Train has passed.

3.25 p.m. Caledonian Cattle Train, Guthrie to Arbroath, **must Stop, and remain at Letham Mill** until the Imperial Train has passed St Vigeans Junction.

3.25 p.m. "Carnyllie" Goods Train, Elliot Junction to Dundee, **must Shunt and remain at Carnoustie** until the Imperial Train has passed.

4.10 p.m. Joint Passenger Train, Arbroath to Dundee East, **must be slowed to a speed not exceeding Ten Miles an hour** while the Imperial Train is passing it on the Down Line.

Should ANY *of the Down Trains be out of Time, they must be shunted into Sidings at such Stations as will ensure their being at a stand 30 minutes before the Imperial Train is due to pass them.*

No Trains or Light Engines, except Passenger Trains, must be allowed to travel between any two Stations on the Up Line from the time the Pilot is due to pass until the Imperial Train has passed between those Stations on the Down Line; and as regards Passenger Trains on the Up Line, they must be slowed to a speed not exceeding ten miles an hour while the Imperial Train is passing them on the Down Line.

Agents and others are required personally to distribute this Notice to their Staff, and every person supplied with a Copy is held responsible to read it carefully through, to note the general information it contains, and to act up to and obey the instructions particularly applicable to himself. No excuse of want of knowledge of these Special Arrangements can be admitted for any failure or neglect of duty. Acknowledge receipt by First Train.

GEO. G. HAMILTON, **Manager.**

8.—**Working of Junctions.**—No Train, Engine, or Vehicle whatever, having to proceed upon the Down Main Line, must be allowed to enter upon the Block Section next to the Junction for at least 30 minutes before the Imperial Train is due to pass the Junction, nor until it has passed the Signal Box in advance of the Junction, in terms of No. 16 of these Instructions; and no Train, Engine, or Vehicle whatever, having to cross the Down Main Line, must be allowed to enter upon the Block Section next to the Junction for at least 30 minutes before the Imperial Train is due, nor until it has passed the Junction.

9.—**Drivers of such Trains as are standing** in Sidings or on adjoining Lines waiting for the passing of the Imperial Train must prevent their Engines from emitting smoke, or making a noise by blowing off steam, or whistling, when the Imperial Train is passing.

10.—**The Brakesmen of all Trains** brought to a stand upon the Lines adjoining that upon which the Imperial Train is travelling will be held responsible for carefully examining the loading of their Trains, directly they come to a stand, to see that nothing is projecting.

11.—**Stationmasters, Goods Agents, Signalmen, Gatekeepers, and others in charge,** must lock their gates, and not allow any vehicle of any kind to enter, or cross the Line, for at least 30 minutes before the Imperial Train is due, nor until it has passed.

12.—**A Platelayer must be stationed** at each Occupation Crossing on the Joint Line to prevent anything coming on to the Line for at least 30 minutes before the Imperial Train is due, and until it has passed.

13.—**Each Foreman Platelayer,** after having examined his length of Line, must station himself at the South end of it and appoint one of his Assistants to the North end; and immediately after the Pilot Engine has passed, these men must walk over the intervening space till they meet each other, so as to ensure that the Line is in every way safe for the passage of the Imperial Train. Each Foreman Platelayer, and each Assistant along the Line, must be provided with Signal Flags and Six Detonating Fog Signals.

14.—**As the Pilot passes each Telegraph Station or Block Telegraph Cabin** its progress must be immediately Telegraphed by Needle Instrument to the next Telegraph Station or Block Telegraph Cabin in the rear; and unless it has been so Telegraphed the Imperial Train must be stopped.

15.—**The passing of the Imperial Train** must also be immediately Telegraphed by Needle Instrument to the next Telegraph Station or Block Telegraph Cabin in the rear.

16.—**Where the Block Telegraph System is in operation,** no Junction Signalman must accept the "Is Line clear?" Signal for any Train or Engine requiring to cross the Down Main Line for at least 30 minutes before the Imperial Train is due, nor until it has passed the Junction; and no Signalman must accept the "Is Line clear?" Signal for any Train or Engine following the Imperial Train until he has received the "Train out of Section" Signal for the Imperial Train from the Signal Box in advance. **Where the Block Telegraph System is not in operation,** the Danger Signals must be kept on until the Signalman has received information by the Needle Instrument that the Imperial Train has passed the Signal Box in advance.

17.—**The Pilot and the Imperial Train** must be worked on the Block Telegraph System where that System is in operation; and in addition thereto, the Special Regulations in Nos. 14, 15, and 16 of these Instructions must be strictly observed.

18.—**Stationmasters, Clerks in charge, and Signalmen** must be **most particular** that the Telegraph is duly attended to during the progress of the Imperial Train, and must take care that it is not used for any other Messages than those connected with the working of that Train and its Pilot.

19.—**Foremen Platelayers must block** all the Facing Points on their respective lengths of Line by wooden keys or wedges before the passing of the Pilot, and must keep them so blocked until the Imperial Train has passed.

20.—**The Agents at all Stations** must be on duty and see that the Instructions herein laid down are strictly observed by the Staff at their respective Stations. They must also arrange that their Staff give as much assistance as possible in keeping Trespassers off the Railway.

The Stations are to be kept quite clear and private while the Imperial Train is passing them; and none of the Public are, under any circumstances, to be admitted to any *of the Stations. The Servants of the Committee are to perform the necessary work on the Platforms without noise; and no cheering or other demonstration must be allowed—the object being that His Imperial Majesty shall be perfectly undisturbed during the journey.*

The Working of the Imperial Train and its Pilot will be performed by the **North British Railway Company,** and the foregoing Regulations will apply to the **Dundee and Arbroath Joint Line** between **Camperdown Junction (Dundee)** and **St Vigeans Junction (Arbroath).**

GEO. G. HAMILTON, **Manager.**

Right: The North British royal train entering Stirling from the north.

Below right: The Caledonian hierarchy in attendance on the royal train at Dunblane in 1914. Donald Matheson, general manager is seventh from the left and William Pickersgill, locomotive superintendent fifth from the left.

Below: Aberdeen Joint Station dressed over-all to receive the royal train. It was vital that the train was stopped with the door of the royal saloon exactly in line with the red carpet.

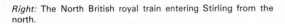

Glasgow & South Western profiles. No 271, *above,* was of the 187 class of 60 engines designed by James Stirling and built by Neilson & Co in 1878. It worked on main line goods and occasional passenger trains when new, but was relegated to secondary duties in later years. No 271 was photographed on the Portpatrick branch in 1915. No 4, *top left,* was one of James Manson's Class 8 4–4–0s which did distinguished work on the Glasgow–Carlisle expresses.

Bottom left: The Manson 4–4–0s of the 336 class were built by Dübs & Co between 1895 and 1899. No 14216 is seen heading a light express near Prestwick in early LMS days.

Below: The Whitelegg Baltics made even lineside laymen turn their heads. They were an impressive spectacle roaring up the Ayrshire coast with a heavy express as No 541 is doing in this picture. But these vast engines, powerful and speedy as they were, arrived in the last months of the South West's existence. To the LMS they were incapable of standardisation and therefore expendable. The longest lived of the class saw only 13 years of service.

6   SOU' WEST SCENES

'Of the three railways that have their terminii in the City of St Mungo that to which the citizens have the warmest side is the Glasgow & South Western. While its neighbours have interests which lead them far away to the east and the north the Glasgow & South Western is pre-eminently the Glasgow system. Its headquarters are here, the different branches converge on Glasgow thereby assisting to swell at once our population and our trade.'

THE BAILIE
(A chauvinistic Glasgow Periodical)

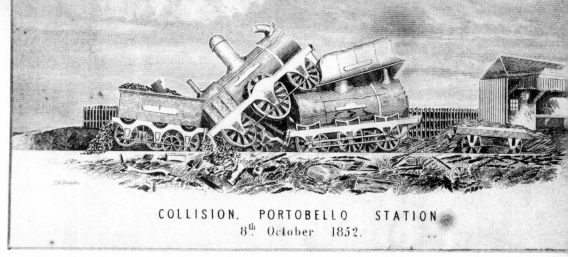

COLLISION. PORTOBELLO STATION
8th October 1852.

Top left: James Stirling's No 471 of 1875 as rebuilt by Manson in 1899.

Above: Cameras were scarce in 1852, but P D Denholm's intriguing woodcut shows the result of a collision between two North British engines at Portobello in October of that year. The artist has seen fit to record the time on the station clock.

7 ACCIDENTS WILL HAPPEN

Bottom left: Manson's No 425 of 1896 as rebuilt by Whitelegg in 1920.

Below: Cameras were not too plentiful in 1872 but a photographer was around to record the aftermath of this boiler explosion at Bridge of Dun on the Caledonian Railway on 23 March. No 503 was built at the Camden Works, Birkenhead in 1857 for the Scottish North Eastern Railway.

Left: Bucksburn station.

The Great North of Scotland Railway served, among other places, the lovely valleys of the Spey and the Dee. The picture *below* shows a Speyside train at Newton Bridge between Craigellachie and Dufftown. *Below left:* The riverside station of Cambus o' May on the Deeside line.

The locomotive superintendent of the GNS from 1890 to 1894 was James Johnson whose father was S W Johnson of the Midland Railway. The previous locomotive superintendent of the GNS, James Manson, had initiated the design of an 0–4–4 tank for the Aberdeen suburban services just before Johnson took over. It was hardly surprising that this engine and Johnson's own first design for the GNS, a 4–4–0 tender engine, should exhibit marked Midland characteristics, No 90 (0–4–4T) and No 80 (4–4–0) were both delivered from Neilson & Co in December 1893. The engines are seen here, rebuilt, at Aberdeen Joint Station as LNER No 6890 (*right*) and No 6880 (*below right*).

Below: Sight-testing signals on the Deeside line.

Above: A small culvert near Carrbridge was considered sufficient to contain the burn that ran through it, but its inadequacy to deal with a sudden spate in July 1922 is evident from the damage shown in this picture.

Below: The Baddengorm Burn, also near Carrbridge, was the scene of the worst disaster on the Highland Railway. The bridge spanning it and part of the down mail were swept away on 18 June 1914.

9 STORM, FLOOD AND TEMPEST

The Highland Railway between Aviemore and Carrbridge crosses a succession of small burns running down from the Monadhliath Mountains. It is a characteristic of these innocuous streams, across which a child could step with ease, that they can turn within minutes into raging torrents.

Right: The Baddengorm Burn disaster as seen by the *Christian Herald.*

THE CHRISTIAN HERALD AND SIGNS OF OUR TIMES

Price 1d. THURSDAY, JULY 2, 1914. 49TH YEAR. No. 27

A Highland Railway Train Falling into a Flooded Gorge.

Below: The restored bridge across Baddengorm Burn and the now subdued insignificant trickle which, as a raging torrent, caused the tragedy.

Immediately to the east of Kirkintilloch station the North British Campsie branch was sandwiched between two layers of water. Above the trains was the Forth & Clyde canal and below them the Luggie Water. These pictures show what happened when the tunnel carrying the Luggie under the line became clogged with melting snow and the stream flowed across the railway.

Above: Kirkintilloch station and goods yard as seen by the watchers on the aqueduct.

Top left: The 5ft wheels of Dugald Drummond's little 4–4–0 tank No 24 barely keep the frames above the water line.

Bottom left: Spectators on the canal aqueduct enjoy the spectacle of a passenger train charging through the flood.

Below: With the Caledonian main line looking like a canal and the platform a pier Drummond 0–6–0 No 691 halts at Perth ticket platform with a passenger train.

Left: The Highland Railway prided itself on its expertise in the deployment and use of mechanical snow-clearing apparatus. But there were times when machines were powerless against the ravages of the elements as on this occasion near Thurso when terraces had to be hand cut out of the hard-frozen snow.

Right: No 71 *Clachnacuddin* and a sister engine in trouble at Killiecrankie after striking a snowdrift on 17 November 1893.

Left: Gone to lunch.

Right: Sandstorms presented problems for railways near the Moray Firth. On occasion the track was completely buried in fine sand during windstorms. The HR civil engineer devised these unique sand blowers which deflected blown sand away from the line on the vulnerable Burghead branch.

Left: Caledonian Railway. A Drummond rebuild of a Conner 2–4–0 and a Jumbo in harness following a strenuous spell of snow ploughing duty.

Above: In the first years of the century several railway boards sought to solve the problem of uneconomical branch lines by employing light steam rail cars. This picture shows one of two such cars operated by the Great North of Scotland Railway. The engine unit had the 0–2–2 wheel arrangement and Walshaerts valve gear and was supplied with steam from a Cochrane vertical boiler. The cars were introduced in November 1905 and after giving a year of unreliable and intermittent service on the St Combs, Lossiemouth, Alford and Old Meldrum branches were withdrawn in November 1906. The engines were scrapped and the boilers put to use as stationery boilers at Inverurie Works and the Palace Hotel, Aberdeen. The bodies were rebuilt as saloons.

10   RAIL CARS

Far right: Sentinel steam rail cars were introduced by the LNER and LMS in the 1920s. Those on the LNER were attractively painted in green and cream and named after stage coaches, a print of the appropriate stage coach being displayed in the saloon. In service the cars were unreliable and fourteen were required to maintain ten services. A Sentinel car is depicted here in Princes Street Gardens.

Right: The diesel railbus was the final attempt in the late 1950s to establish rail car travel. It failed like its predecessors because of the unreliability of the vehicle, and because the traffic for which it was suited was not really enough to justify a railway of any sort.

Below: The body section of a former GNSR rail car in LNER days.

NEW
DIESEL RAILBUS

between

LUGTON
BARRMILL

and

BEITH (TOWN)

MONDAYS to SATURDAYS
6th April to 14th June, 1959
or until further notice

TRAVEL BY THE MODERN RAILWAY

 BRITISH RAILWAYS

*for service and special
cheap day fares see other side*

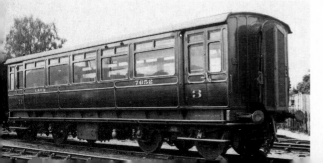

11   GLIMPSES OF THE CALEDONIAN

Above: The engine that made the reputation of the Caledonian—McIntosh's Dunalastair. One of the class leaves Glasgow Central.

CR No 119 and 120 were 7ft 2in 2–4–0s designed by Benjamin Conner and built in 1868 by Neilson & Co as Nos 468 and 469. *Top left:* No 119 as rebuilt by Dugald Drummond and, *centre left,* No 120 as rebuilt by Lambie.

Some of Conner's fast 6ft 2in goods engines were rebuilt by Drummond and put into passenger service. No 480 built in 1868 is seen, *below,* at Glasgow Central and No 474 built in 1867 is entering Buchanan Street station, Glasgow, *bottom left,* on a passenger train.

'While the Caledonian Railway policy is distinguished by the dash and adventure characteristic of the Second City of the British Empire the old fashioned stay-at-home methods of working adopted by the North British authorities seem to belong, as it were by right to the dullness and formalism peculiar to the capital and all that pertains to it. The Caledonian is new, eager and daring, the North British is old and safe. The one suits a constituency of bustling merchants, the other one of steady-going somewhat antiquated lawyers.'

THE BAILIE 1882

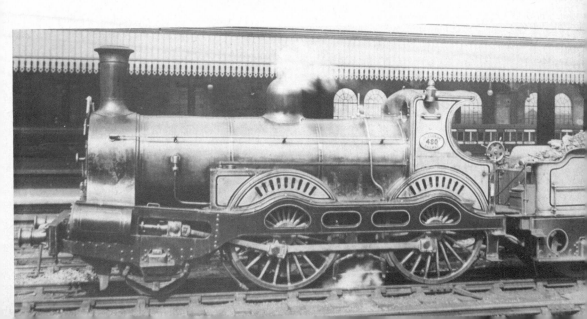

The Wemyss Bay tanks. Pickersgill's 4–6–2 tanks of 1917 seen, *right,* in action on their 'home' ground shortly after the grouping. These engines are thought of mainly in connection with the Clyde coast trains, but their work ranged from stopping trains on the CR Edinburgh–Glasgow line, football specials through the tunnels of the Glasgow Central Railway and banking at Beattock. *Above:* A Wemyss Bay tank in the unlikely company of an NB Atlantic at Carlisle.

Top left: A Jumbo at Aberdeen (old) station.

Above: No 898 of the 900 class (unofficially known as Dunalastair III) waiting at Carlisle to take over a northbound train.

Bottom left: A Pickersgill 300 class 0–6–0 of 1916 still in CR livery heads a main line goods in the mid 1920s.

Below: No 50 *Sir James Thompson,* one of the two Class 49 4–6–0s built by McIntosh in 1903, passes Etterby with a southbound express.

56

Above: Shed staff at Lochgorm, Inverness pose around a well-turned-out 'Yankee' still sporting its South American chimney.

12   HIGHLAND POSES

Above: A shopman beside a Castle under repair at Lochgorm.

Below: HR No 73 *Snaigow* festooned with Highland lassies at Lochgorm soon after its delivery from R&W Hawthorn Leslie & Co in 1917. This large, powerful 4–4–0 and its sister engine *Durn* were built for the Inverness–Wick line, then under severe strain because of heavy wartime traffic to Scapa Flow.

Right: Staff at Dingwall pose beside HR No 53, built at Inverness by David Jones as an 0–4–4 saddle tank in 1890 and rebuilt with side tanks and a Drummond boiler in 1901.

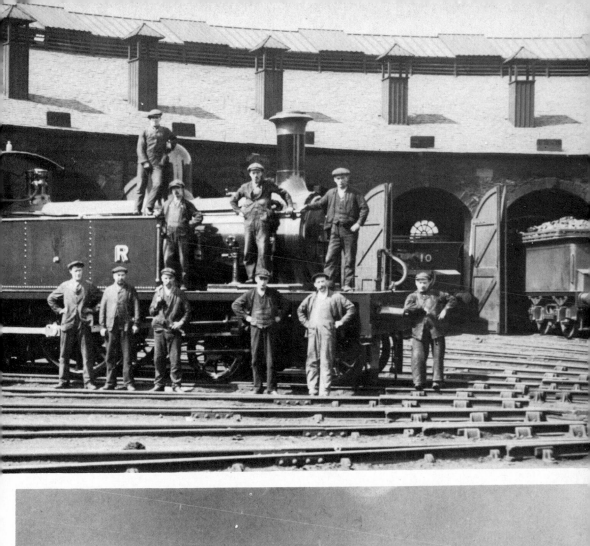

Above: NBR No 155, looking very spruce at Anstruther in 1887, was built at St Margaret Works, Edinburgh eight years earlier from spare parts and the recycled remains of old engines originally supplied to the Edinburgh, Perth & Dundee Railway in 1856. No 155 survived until 1914.

13 RAILWAYMEN

Below: Itinerant photographers ranged the country visiting railway communities and taking pictures of proud railwaymen. A photographer from Barnsley took this picture of NBR No 2 in which the standard tableau of driver, fireman, guard and shunter has been augmented by the addition of the local stationmaster, albeit standing apart from the main group. Note the almost balletic placing of the hands. No 2 was built at Cowlairs by Thomas Wheatley in 1871 and appears here as rebuilt by Matthew Holmes some 20 years later.

Above: Stewarton station on the Glasgow, Barrhead & Kilmarnock Joint Line in the 1870s.

Below: Braidwood, Caledonian Railway.

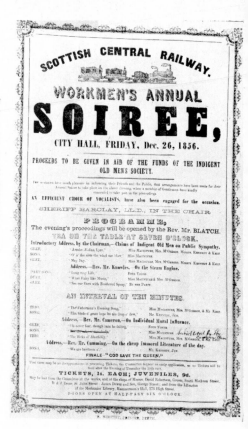

Below: Some of the old railway companies maintained private fire brigades recruited from staff. Membership was voluntary and usually unpaid, but the firemen were given free travel passes for themselves and families at a time when passes were the perquisite of the upper echelons of the railway hierarchy. The railway fire-brigades, like the one at Inverurie Works of the Great North of Scotland Railway pictured here, would not have disgraced in turnout and equipment the fire service of a sizeable town. The firemen could be summoned day and night by a distinctive blast on the works hooter. The fire horn was as much a part of railway communities as was the wail of the disaster hooter in colliery villages.

Far left: W Sim was fortunate enough to be invited to the directors' reception in 1898.

Right: Staff at Keith GNSR.

Left: The programme of the Workmen's Annual Soiree, Scottish Central Railway, 1856.

The bowler hat remained the foreman's badge of office through the ages. *Below:* Officers and foremen pose in front of No 554 about 1913. Turning shop staff at St Rollox in 1926, *right*, are obviously pleased to announce their identity.

14 PASSENGERS

Right: The atmosphere of a Victorian country station is splendidly captured in this study of Auchtermuchty in Fife.

Bottom right: Passengers at Peebles await the arrival of the Galashiels train.

Bottom left: Edwardian travellers on the Campbeltown & Machrihanish Railway.

Below: This is how a Dundee newspaper saw travel on the North British in 1902. Note the 'crossed snails' emblem on the smokebox door. The caption to the cartoon read 'At the annual concert of the North British Railway employees at Methil the other night—Mr W F Jackson, general manager of the North British Railway presiding—Mr Masterton in proposing a vote of thanks to the Committee, propounded the query—Where in history is the North British Railway first mentioned? Answer—in Genesis, where can be read the history of creation of all creeping things!'

CHAPTER FROM RAILWAY HISTORY

15 IN AND AROUND EDINBURGH

Edinburgh has something more exciting than fairies at the bottom of its garden—trains. Surely Princes Street Gardens furnish the most elegant viewing point in the country. In steam days locomotives passed in continuous pageant under the Castle battlements and through the Mound tunnels on their way to and from Waverley station and Haymarket shed.

Above: A Director passes Princes Street Gardens at the head of a Glasgow express.

Left: A Shire, Director and V1 in a lively line up at the Mound tunnels.

Left: Waverley west-end pilots emerge from the Mound tunnels on parallel shunt moves.

Below: One of Gresley's V1 2–6–2 tanks, built specially for Scottish suburban work, is seen at speed sprinting away from Edinburgh near Haymarket.

Left: LNER A4 No 9 *Union of South Africa* and an A2 Pacific sandwich a V1 tank as the trio move towards the station to take up duty.

Top left: Princes Street station interior.

Bottom left: A glistening Lambie 4—4—0 at Princes Street station.

Above: Photographers who were privileged to take pictures on the Forth Bridge tended to concentrate on the lordly expresses forgetting that the bridge was also host to humble Edinburgh commuter trains. Class V1 2—6—2 tank No 2916 is seen crossing the bridge with a Dunfermline—Edinburgh train.

16 LOCOMOTIVE BUILDERS TO THE WORLD

Glasgow was a world centre of the locomotive-building trade. The Board of Trade returns for 1899 showed that three out of every four men engaged in the industry within the United Kingdom worked in Glasgow.

Top left: The heart of any locomotive-building establishment was the drawing office. There generations of locomotives were conceived and many thousands of drawings prepared. The draughtsmen were the elite of a railway community. A job in the drawing office was much coveted, but only the cleverest boys were chosen to be apprentices. This picture shows a corner of the drawing office at the North British Locomotive Company headquarters.

Bottom left: A new engine for the Egyptian State Railways leaves Hyde Park Works en route for the docks.

Below: There was a carnival atmosphere in the streets as an engine made its way to the Clyde. As the traction engines ease their charge between a wartime surface air raid shelter and the pavement housewives look on from their tenement windows, and children watch in wonder.

Above: A locomotive for the Malayan Railway crosses Sauchiehall Street in the heart of Glasgow.

Below: NBL locomotives and Hurst Nelson carriages loaded ready for dispatch.

Above: A 'Bel' ship arrives at an Eastern port ready to discharge its cargo.

Below: A brand new B1 for BR ready to leave the works.

17 THE ROYAL SCOT

The big event in the Anglo-Scottish transport scene in the 1920s was the introduction by the LMS of the Royal Scot class locomotives on the Euston–Glasgow service and the bestowing of the title The Royal Scot to the principal day train. The new train was advertised under the splendid slogan 'Punctuality is the Politeness of Kings.' The first 50 Royal Scot engines were built in Glasgow. S P B Mais, a prominent writer and broadcaster of the time, described their livery as 'a dawn-like blush that suffuses her whole surface.'

Above: The Royal Scot leaves Glasgow for London.

Top right: The Royal Scot at speed on the outskirts of the city.

Bottom right: Royal Scot class No 6399 *Fury* was given a Schmidt high pressure boiler delivering steam at 900lb/sq in. It left Hyde Park Works on a trial trip on 10 February 1930, but had got only as far as Carstairs when a high pressure steam pipe fractured causing the death of an inspector who was travelling on the footplate. The experiment was abandoned and the engine was later rebuilt as a more conventional Royal Scot although with a taper boiler and other detail differences. As *British Legion*, No 6170 served for many years.

Left: In 1928 the LMS placed in service on the Royal Scot service new first class coaches, usually one in each of the Glasgow and Edinburgh portions, with part side corridor and part open saloon seating for dining purposes. The compartments had only four seats so that everyone had a corner, and each of the three compartments had individual decorative treatment with different seating moquettes and woodgrain finishes from British Empire timbers.

Top left: Until the second world war the two principal daytime Anglo-Scottish services to London on the West Coast route, other than the short lived Coronation Scot, included portions for Glasgow, Edinburgh and Aberdeen, although according to season the various portions sometimes ran as independent through trains between Scotland and London. When combined, the portions were attached or detached at Symington. Here former Caledonian 4–4–0 No 14455 arrives at Symington with the southbound Edinburgh portion of the Mid-day Scot in 1929. *Left:* The main train from Glasgow stands at Symington behind Royal Scot 4–6–0 No 6123 *Royal Irish Fusilier*.

Above: Surmounting Scotland's heavy gradients was thirsty work for locomotives. When the LMS was reorganising its West Coast services in the 1920s the conclusion was reached that the water troughs south of Carlisle, which made possible long distance non-stop runs, had their value neutralised by the absence of troughs north of the Border. In advocating water troughs in Scotland the Chief General Superintendent wrote, 'As time goes on the result of providing these water troughs will lessen the necessity of building express passenger engines with large tenders and water tanks. The LNE Company are very alive to strengthening their position in respect of the traffic between England and Scotland and it is very desirable that we should not delay in coming to a decision.' Troughs were provided at Strawfrank south of Carstairs and near New Cumnock on the former G&SW line.

18   ANGLO-SCOTTISH DE LUXE

In 1938 both the LMS and LNER vied with each other in the introduction of new luxury express services between London and Scotland. Both were worked by streamlined locomotives and both had coaches which were ostensibly better than normal stock used on other services. The LNER came off best with its new coaches for the Coronation train which were built specially and included many new features including sound insulation, pressure ventilation and smart interior decor and seating layout. There was also an observation car. The LMS merely refurbished existing coaches of the latest pattern for its Coronation Scot trains and painted them in a striking blue and silver livery. *Above,* the southbound Coronation Scot passes Oxenholme in 1939. *Below,* the LNER Coronation speeds through Welwyn Garden City bound for Edinburgh in 1939.

"THE CORONATION"

THE FIRST STREAMLINE TRAIN
KING'S CROSS FOR SCOTLAND

THE "BEAVER-TAIL"

OBSERVATION CAR

ON THIS TRAIN

giving an uninterrupted view of the receding scenery as the

train progresses, is available for the use of all

passengers at a charge of

ONE SHILLING PER PERIOD OF ONE HOUR

at the times shown overleaf

TICKETS OBTAINABLE FROM THE ATTENDANT

Again the LNER scored on the quality of its publicity material for its Coronation service and with its slogan 'Kings Cross for Scotland. *Left,* is the card giving details of the Observation Car and below sample menus, *left,* luncheon on the Coronation Scot and *right,* dinner on the Coronation, in both cases in the third class cars.

Luncheon
3/6

Crème Andalouse

—

Whiting au Gratin

Roast Beef   Horseradish Sauce
Baked & Boiled Potatoes
Green Vegetables
or
Assorted Cold Meats
Salad

Orange Custard Pudding
or
Vanilla Ice

Biscuits   Cheese   Salad

Coffee, per Cup, 4d.

THIRD CLASS   AFTERNOON TEA. 1/3   26 8 38.

The L M S Official Time Table and the A. B. C. Railway Guide can be consulted and Writing Paper and Envelopes obtained on application to the Conductor.

In the general interest Passengers are requested to refrain from smoking immediately prior to and during the service of meals. Passengers are requested to see that their bills are written out in their presence, and not to pay any money until the bill has been presented.

MENU

DINNER 4/6

English or Scotch Meat
Only Served on this Car

Cantaloupe Melon
or
Potage St. Germaine

Trout Portugaise

Devilled Chicken and Pimientos
or
Roast Saddle Mutton   Red Currant Jelly
Runner Beans   Duchesse Potatoes

Peach Tartlette
Creme Renversee

Cheese etc.

Coffee 4d.

Friday, September 2, 1938   Third-Class
A LA CARTE

SOUPS			GRILLS		
Potage St. Germaine	...	0 6	Chop, Steak or Cutlets	... ...	3 0
If not followed by a second course			(Above served with Vegetables)		
per portion		1 0			
			COLD MEATS		
FISH			Chicken and Ham with Salad	...	3 0
Trout Portugaise	... ...	2 0	SWEETS		
with Potatoes			As per Menu... ... per portion		0 6
			Fruit Salad and Cream per portion		1 0
MEAT DISHES (Hot)					
Devilled Chicken and Pimientos	...	3 0			
Roast Saddle Mutton Red Currant Jelly		2 6	Dessert ... ... per portion		1 0
(Above served with Vegetables)			Rolls or Bread and Butter		0 3
			Roll or Biscuits, Butter and Cheese		
SUNDRIES			per portion		0 6
Cantaloupe Melon	... ...	1 0	Sandwiches per round		0 8

The Company will be obliged if patrons desirous of making any comments regarding the catering or service on this car will write to The Hostels Superintendent, Southern Area London and North Eastern Railway, Liverpool Street Station, London, E.C.2.

VISIT THE EMPIRE EXHIBITION, GLASGOW
OPEN MAY TO OCTOBER

SEAT PLAN OF "THE CORONATION"

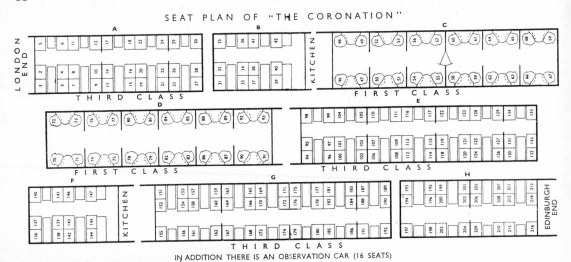

Above: The seating plan of the LNER Coronation.

A feature of the LNER Coronation coaches was the arrangement of seats in the open first class accommodation with each group of four single armchairs partitioned off in alcoves. This photograph (*below*) portrays the very similar West Riding stock but the effect other than the detailed decor was the same. *Left,* is the interior of the observation car with the end observation window behind the photographer.

19 THE GEORGE BENNIE RAILPLANE

Above: A general view of the George Bennie Railplane seen on the short length of track built above the LNER Milngavie branch. A platform was built at one end of the test track. *Below:* The interior of the George Bennie Railplane, rather reminiscent of Pullman cars in its appointments, even to the table lamp and with its three-arc ceiling giving an impression of the clerestory roof of turn of the century carriages.

TUNNELS

British Rail admit to having 110 tunnels in the Scottish Region. At first sight the list looks formidable, but of the imposing total only nine are over 1000 yards long, 77 are less than 500 yards and of these 41 are less than 200 yards. In spite of its mountainous character Scotland has few notable tunnels. On the whole of the Highland Railway there were only three tunnels, all occurring within a few miles—Murthly, Inver and Killiecrankie—and their combined lengths totalled only 1032 yards. The GNS had four tunnels—Schoolhill and Hutcheon Street in Aberdeen, Aboyne and Aberlour—with a total length of 695 yards. Scottish engineers were more concerned with burrowing under urban areas than boring through mountains. Of the 24 miles 300 yards of railway tunnels in Scotland no fewer than 14 miles 236 yards are under town and city streets. Glasgow alone accounts for 9 miles 542 yards of tunnel.

Right: One of the notable Scottish main lines now no longer with us, the North British Waverley route from Edinburgh to Carlisle. It crossed the Southern Uplands nearly as high as the competing West Coast route, with a summit at Whitrope of 970ft. Class V2 2–6–2 No 60836 heads north on the Waverley route near Whitrope with an enthusiast special from Euston to Aberdeen on 3 September 1966, three years before the line closed.

TUNNELS OVER 500 YARDS

Name of Tunnel	Location	Length (Yards)
Anderston Cross	Anderston Cross–Glasgow Green	2,800
Newton Street	Greenock West–Fort Matilda	2,111
Drumlanrig	Sanquhar–Carronbridge	1,395
London Road	Parkhead–Bridgeton Cross	1,300
Moncrieff	Perth–Hilton Junction	1,220
Whitrope	Riccarton Jct–Shankend	1,208
Charing Cross	Queen Street–Charing Cross	1,096
Scotland Street	Waverley–Heriothill	1,052
Haymarket South	Waverley–Haymarket	1,009
Cowlairs	Queen Street–Cowlairs	999
Haymarket North	Waverley–Haymarket	992
Fairlie	Fairlie–Largs	971
Falkirk	Falkirk–Polmont	845
Tamshill	Maryhill–Possil	808
Bishopton	Bishopton–Langbank	770
Dalmarnock Road	Bridgeton Cross–Dalmarnock	766
Kelvinhaugh	Partick Central–Stobcross	755
Finnieston	Charing Cross–Partickhill	742
Union Street	Greenock Princes Pier–Lynedoch Street	718
Balgray	Maryhill–Kelvinside	700
Mossgiel	Hurlford–Mauchline	684
High Street	Queen Street–High Street	681
Dock Street	Dundee–West Ferry	628
Dalreoch	Dalreoch–Cardross	603
Kippenross	Dunblane–Bridge of Allan	600
St Leonards	Duddingston–St Leonards	572
North Queensferry	North Queensferry–Inverkeithing	569
Inver	Inchmagranachan–Dunkeld	538
Pinmore	Pinmore–Girvan	534
Glenfarg	Glenfarg–Bridge of Earn	517
Canning Street	Bridgeton Cross–Glasgow Green	510
Glenfarg North	Glenfarg–Bridge of Earn	507
Stobcross	Anderston Cross–Stobcross	500

SUMMITS

The fact that tunnels were eschewed in the hill regions of Scotland meant that the engineers took their lines over mountain passes. The land abounded in long, steep gradients and spectacular summits. If the Highland Railway boasted only three short tunnels it also had three exciting summits.

Summit	Remarks	Height in Feet
Wanlockhead	The highest point in the United Kingdom reached by a standard gauge railway occurred between Leadhills and Wanlockhead on the Leadhills & Wanlockhead Light Railway.	1498
Druimuachdar	The highest point on the Highland Railway and the highest point in the United Kingdom reached by a main line. This, the original Highland main line came into use on 9 September 1863	1484
Corrour	Highest point on the North British Railway situated between Rannoch and Tulloch near the northern edge of Rannoch Moor, West Highland line.	1350
Slochd Mhuic	In building the direct line from Aviemore to Inverness via Carr Bridge the Highland had to cross high bleak moorland the summit of which is at Slochd.	1315
Dava	This summit occurred where the original Highland main line crossed the ridge between the valleys of the Findhorn and the Spey. The line (Aviemore–Forres) is now closed.	1052
Tyndrum	Situated on the county march between Argyllshire and Perthshire north of Tyndrum, West Highland line.	1024
Beattock	This famous summit on the Caledonian main line was a mighty obstacle to steam-hauled trains for 120 years. Now the electrics soar over it as if it did not exist.	1016
Whitrope	Summit of Waverley Route situated between Riccarton Junction and Shankend.	970
Chirmorie	The highest point on the Glasgow & South Western Railway between Barrhill and Glenwhilly on the Girvan–Stranraer line.	690
New Cumnock	The highest point on the G&SW main line (Glasgow to Carlisle) between Old Cumnock and New Cumnock.	616
Kennethmont	The highest point on the Great North of Scotland occurred between Woodhouse and Kennethmont on the main line.	594
Blackford	The summit at Blackford was more lethal than its modest elevation suggested. It is on the former Caledonian high speed line between Stirling and Perth and presented problems to many a heavily laden express.	422

TEN NOTABLE SCOTTISH ENGINES

The Conner 2–2–2. In 1862 a great International Exhibition was held at South Kensington. That was the year in which Walter Neilson established his Hyde Park works in Glasgow. Just down the road from Hyde Park were the almost new St Rollox works of the Caledonian Railway presided over by Benjamin Conner who had been Neilson's works manager at his old works at Stobcross. Neilson was determined to send an engine to the Exhibition and Conner agreed that Neilson should build one of his spectacular 8ft 2in 2–2–2 express engines for the show. The engine was duly turned out, painted in Caledonian livery and sent to London. For the first time Londoners witnessed the glory of Caledonian blue. *The Engineer* thought the engine 'one of the finest examples of locomotive construction in the Exhibition.' So did Said Pasha, Viceroy of Egypt, who bought it and took it to Egypt where it ran for 35 years. In 1932 the engine appeared on a stamp issued by the Egyptian Government to celebrate the International Railway Congress.

The Drummond 476 class. Conner was not the only Scottish locomotive engineer to get an engine on a stamp. A similar honour fell to Dugald Drummond whose Abbotsford class graced one of the four stamps issued to commemorate the 150th anniversary of the Stockton & Darlington Railway in 1975. It was a worthy choice. Drummond produced his engine in 1876 to meet his company's pressing need for increased power on the Waverley Route and especially to cope with the new Midland Anglo-Scottish expresses. The old engines were slow and needed assistance on the banks. The 476 class could run the 98 miles between Carlisle and Edinburgh with 117-ton loads in 2hr 10min burning only 28 pounds of coal per mile in the process, 'a wonderfully good result,' commented *Engineering*. The engine put Drummond's feet on the ladder of fame.

No 123 was in a class by itself—literally. Of 4–2–2 wheel formation, it was Neilson & Company's entry in the International Exhibition of Industry, Science and Art held in Edinburgh in 1886, although Neilson himself had been ousted from the firm by then. (Walter Neilson submitted his own entry, a 4–4–0 for the Highland Railway, from his own new Clyde Locomotive Works.) No 123 was finished in Caledonian livery and looked in most respects a Drummond engine—Drummond was locomotive superintendent of the Caledonian at that time—but Edward Snowball, Neilson & Company's chief draughtsman declared in print that the engine was solely the design of the proprietor of Hyde Park who, of course, was James Reid. The statement never was contradicted. After the exhibition No 123 joined the Caledonian stud. It was the only engine used by the company during the 1888 Race to Edinburgh. Later it worked on secondary passenger trains and when required acted as Royal Train pilot. The engine re-emerged in its former glory in 1958 to run for several years on special trains. It is now in the Glasgow Museum of Transport.

About **No 124** there was no ambiguity. While Neilson & Company were building No 123 the rival firm of Dübs & Co. were building No 124 for the same Exhibition. The engine was one of the 66 class of 4–4–0 which Drummond had built to handle the principal expresses of the Caledonian. It was unique in having a valve gear invented by a boyhood friend of Drummond's, Archibald Bryce Douglas, and hitherto employed only in marine engineering. No 124 (like No 123) won a gold medal at the Exhibition and subsequently was put into traffic on the Caledonian. The Bryce Douglas valve gear was not a success and was soon removed. The engine proved to be one of the best performers in Caledonian express service. After a long spell on the heaviest Anglo-

Scottish expresses it was chosen to handle the prestige *Arran Boat Express* on the opening of the Caledonian pier at Ardrossan.

Hercules was the first engine built at the Cowlairs works of the Edinburgh & Glasgow Railway and at the time was claimed to be the most powerful engine in the world. For two years the E & G had been pulling trains up Cowlairs Incline on the end of a hemp rope. Breakages and delays were endemic. William Paton designed *Hercules* to demonstrate that trains could be hauled up a 1 in 42 incline by adhesion alone, a concept not generally accepted. It was a six-coupled tank engine weighing 26½ tons. It had hot water jets in front of the wheels and cold water jets behind the wheels to clean greasy rail surfaces. There were sandboxes under the control of the fireman. *Hercules* performed well and cut the cost of operating the incline by two thirds. But the blast from the chimney as the engine roared up through the tunnel damaged the fabric and after three years rope haulage, but using an improved rope, was restored.

The **Dunalastair 4–4–0** of the Caledonian Railway was the engine that put a 60mph start to stop timing in Bradshaw for the first time. J. F. McIntosh produced the engine at St Rollox in 1896 as a stop gap until a more powerful engine could be built to handle the increasing loads. In appearance it differed little from its Drummond predecessors, but its bigger, higher-pitched boiler gave it a more powerful look. In practice the engine could pull twice the load of the older engines and keep time without assistance. The railway press quickly became aware that something important had happened at St Rollox. The name *Dunalastair* became a name to ponder in the railway world and the activities of Mr McIntosh were watched with interest. A later version of the *Dunalastair* was adopted as a standard express passenger engine on the Belgian railways.

No 49 and No 50, McIntosh 4–6–0s for the Caledonian were, when they appeared in 1903, the largest and heaviest locomotives in Britain. They were sensational. The Caledonian went all out to sell the locomotives to the public as airlines in another age were to sell airliners. The engines were works of art. They were given six coats of paint and three of varnish. The company's initials in unusually large gold letters were emblazoned on the tender and an ornate coat of arms was hand-painted on the leading engine splasher. So great was interest in the engines that large crowds gathered at Glasgow Central station to see them depart. At Carlisle police had to be called out to control the crowds who came to the station to witness their movements. A fine oil painting of No 50 on an Anglo-Scottish express can be seen in the Glasgow Museum of Transport.

The **Sou' West Baltics** Robert Whitelegg's massive 4–6–4 tanks came to the Glasgow & South Western in the last ten months of the company's life. They were their designer's swan song. He had been locomotive superintendent of the London, Tilbury & Southend, but internal politics had thwarted his ambition to operate a great express engine. The G & SW gave him his chance. His Baltics were powerful in performance and overpowering in appearance. They did well on the coast expresses. But they had innovations that gave trouble and the LMS had no patience with them. The six majestic giants had disappeared from the scene 13 years after their first appearance.

The **Jones Goods** of the Highland Railway in 1894 was the first 4–6–0 engine in Britain. The Highland found itself taking over ever increasing loads from the southern companies at Perth and, being faced with the task of getting the trains over the system's gruelling summits, David Jones's bold answer was to adopt the hitherto untried (in Britain) 4–6–0 wheel arrangement. The resulting engine was the most powerful engine in Britain when built. Of the 15 engines of the class No 103 is the survivor and can be seen in the Glasgow Museum of Transport.

The **North British Atlantic** was Scotland's only 4–4–2 tender engine. It was introduced in 1906 mainly, like Drummond's Abbotsford class of 1876, to cut out expensive double heading on the Waverley Route, but it immediately became the subject of bitter in-fighting among the North British hierarchy. James Bell, the civil engineer, claimed that the engine was spreading the road and was dangerous at high speeds, and the management was reluctant to accept the assurances of the locomotive superintendent, W. P. Reid, that it was not. Raven of the North Eastern and Ivatt of the Great Northern were called in to evaluate the locomotive's performance. In the end Bell was shown to have been over-cautious and once the engines were given their head they proved their worth.

FIFTY SCOTTISH RAILWAY PERSONALITIES

Scotland, in spite of its size, was rich in railway personalities. Here are 50 thumb-nail sketches of people, from passengers to chairmen of companies, who have adorned the railway scene.

Alexander Allan gave up a promising career at Crewe to become the first locomotive superintendent of the Scottish Central Railway. His Crewe type engines dominated most of the lines north of Stirling for a time, but he was dropped by the Caledonian when it absorbed the Scottish Central in 1865 and he passed into relative obscurity. At the time of his death in Scarborough many years later he was conducting experiments on stabilisers for ships.

John Anderson, secretary and manager of the Callander & Oban Railway, virtually created the railway single-handed. He sold shares round the doors after the fashion of a brush salesman, cajoled hoteliers into promoting railway excursions and advertising them at their own expense and suggested to the Astronomer Royal that he furnish a statement to the effect that a resort on the C & O had a better climate that a rival resort on the Caledonian.

Sir William Arrol from a humble beginning as a mender of porridge pots became a bridge builder of international repute. He was responsible for two of the world's most famous railway bridges—the Forth and the (second) Tay.

C. R. H. Bonn before World War 1 tried to interest the North British Locomotive Co Ltd in diesel propulsion for locomotives. His proposal was considered at board level, but the NBL hierarchy, thirled to steam, saw nothing of practical value in Bonn's proposals.

Sir Thomas Bouch came to Scotland from the north of England in 1849 as manager of the Edinburgh & Northern Railway. He got off to a good start by putting on the Forth the world's first roll-on roll-off train ferry, a concept which the railway directors agreed succeeded beyond the most sanguine expectations. Bouch left railway service in 1851 and set up business in Edinburgh as a consulting engineer, a profession he was to follow for 30 years. He specialised in building cheap railway lines for small independent companies, the Peebles Railway, the Leven Railway, and the Crieff Junction Railway among others. Too late his clients discovered that they had got no more than they had paid for—cheap lines that soon required expensive rebuilding. Bouch moved on to the grandiose with proposals for two massive bridges across the Forth, a three mile bridge at Blackness and a suspension bridge a mile and a half long at Queensferry. His Tay Bridge, opened on 31 May 1878, collapsed on 28 December 1879, blame for the disaster being placed mainly on Bouch's faulty design and lack of supervision. His last bridge, that over the South Esk at Montrose, was dismantled before a train had run over it.

R. W. Campbell, author, during World War I created a popular Glasgow character in Spud Tamson of the HLI. Urged to produce a comparable peacetime character Campbell came up with Snooker Tam, a porter at one of the stations on the Cathcart Circle. *Snooker Tam of the Cathcart Railway*, one of the best-loved railway books ever published, contained humorous and shrewd observations on railway life and on Glasgow commuters as seen through the eyes of a humble porter.

R. E. Charlwood was an English enthusiast and writer whose articles in the *Railway Magazine* and elsewhere did much to illumine the Scottish railway scene. On his retirement he elected to live—and die—at Carr Bridge beside the Highland line. He is buried in the cemetery at that place.

Frédéric Chopin was a patron of the early Scottish railways. He travelled on the Scottish Central in October 1848 shortly after the line was opened. His destination was Dunblane and the home of the Stirlings who had been prominent in the promotion of the line. The 'kind Scotch lady' of Chopin's diaries was related to John Stirling of Kippendavie who was to become a director of the Caledonian and chairman of the North British.

Designer with his engine: Peter Drummond (right) stands beside Highland 4–4–0 No 144 *Blair Castle* prepared for a press trip to the Far North.

Robert Currer was befriended when a schoolboy by Colonel McDonald of Powderhall, one of the original directors of the Caledonian, and was given a clerkship in March 1848, a month after the opening of the line. He was to have a long and varied association with the company. He was for a period in charge of timetables and when the Forth & Clyde Canal was taken over by the Caledonian he was made manager of the waterway. In 1879, as traffic manager, he 'altered the mode of block telegraphing to the affirmative principle' an innovation that was made the subject of a lecture given by the great Professor Thompson (Lord Kelvin) at the Belfast meeting of the British Association. He is also credited with having introduced the electric train staff for single line working. In another sphere he pioneered a system of cheap excursions which was copied by many other lines.

Robert Davidson, an Aberdonian, in 1839 built an electric locomotive capable of carrying two passengers across a rough wooden floor. A more powerful version of the locomotive weighing five tons was tested at Eastfield on the Edinburgh &

Glasgow Railway in September 1842 and achieved a speed of four miles per hour. The locomotive, however, could not carry sufficient batteries to enable it to maintain this speed over an economical distance. Davidson had the right idea, but he was before his time.

Charles Dickens, sick and near his end, made his last railway journey from Edinburgh to London in the Great Northern Railway Royal Day Saloon which had been specially requested by Mason, the general manager of the North British. Bedding and furniture from Mason's house was provided for the journey. Dickens was fascinated by rail travel, but in his declining years his doctor gave 'long and frequent railway journeys' as one of the two causes of his illness.

Andrew Dougall was one of Scotland's greatest railway administrators. He nursed the constituents of the Highland Railway into existence and did more than any other man to make that company what it became—the greatest commercial enterprise in the Highlands. Such was his power that he at times took and implemented major policy decisions—like floating a new share issue—and told his board afterwards.

Dugald Drummond, arguably the greatest of the Scottish locomotive superintendents, first came to notice as a youthful but ambitious foreman at Cowlairs in Edinburgh & Glasgow days. By 1875, and still only 35 years old, he was locomotive superintendent of the North British. He made his name with the 476 express engine for the Waverley route. In 1882 he transferred to the Caledonian where he promptly repeated his success. By 1890 he was a giant among locomotive engineers and poised for even greater fame. But he made the mistake of resigning from the Caledonian to take over the management of a proposed locomotive building plant in Australia. When the project fell through he accepted an invitation to be locomotive superintendent of the London & South Western Railway at a salary much less than he had been receiving from the Caledonian. Some of his former sparkle seemed to go out of him, for his English engines never attained the prestige of their Scottish counterparts.

Peter Drummond never seemed to emerge completely from the long shadow cast by his illustrious elder brother. He was at Cowlairs when Dugald was there in 1875. He was works manager at St Rollox when his brother was locomotive superintendent of the Caledonian. Dugald's move to England did little to lessen the fraternal bond. When Peter went to the Highland as locomotive superintendent (Dugald had been there before him as works manager to Stroudley) his brother continued to influence his work. Dugald was dead by the time Peter became locomotive superintendent of the Glasgow & South Western, but even so many features of his engines continued to owe more to Eastleigh than to Kilmarnock practice.

Henry Dübs was brought to Scotland by Walter Neilson in the belief that Dübs' influence with English locomotive superintendents would result in Neilson & Co obtaining English orders. Neilson, however, did not consider Dübs' business methods 'honest and honourable.' He described him as a poor engineer and 'a most pigheaded German and most difficult to get on

with.' The association between Dübs and Neilson was short-lived. Dübs left Neilson & Co to start his rival Glasgow Locomotive Works.

John Duncan, blacksmith, in 1886 designed an apparatus by means of which single line tablets could be exchanged safely at speeds up to 50mph. The apparatus was introduced on the Great North of Scotland Railway by James Manson then locomotive superintendent of the company, and who has been credited with its invention. The 'Manson' tablet exchanger was widely used on single line railways.

Sir John Fowler is best known as the designer (with Sir Benjamin Baker) of the Forth Bridge. He had large estates in the Highlands and had an interest in railway development in the region. He was for a time a director of the Dingwall & Skye Railway. He was also consulting engineer to the abortive Garve & Ullapool Railway and, in his later years, consulting engineer to the Highland Railway.

William Graham was a man of many parts. He was a fireman on the Edinburgh & Glasgow and a driver on the North British. He was one of the first amateur photographers in Scotland and for the last 20 years of his life he was a professional photographer. He was a writer and a pioneer in railway Red Cross work. His scrapbooks and many of his original photographic plates are preserved in the Mitchell Library, Glasgow.

Sir Nigel Gresley, one of Britain's most famous locomotive engineers, and designer of several classes specifically for Scottish duties (the K4s for the West Highland and the P2s for the Edinburgh-Aberdeen route) was Scottish by birth. He was born in Edinburgh.

Richard Hodgson, MP for Northumberland, did more than anyone else to build up and consolidate the North British. As chairman he was ruthless in his efforts to keep the Caledonian at bay, and at the same time he systematically acquired independent lines on behalf of his company. In the end his rash financial exploits nearly destroyed the company. 'I have not served the company for money,' he said in parting, 'it has been a matter of love with me.'

Matthew Holmes, locomotive superintendent of the North British, a man of quiet dignity, perhaps was the best loved of the Scottish superintendents. On one occasion his staff sent him the following telegram. 'Members of the locomotive staff toast enthusiastic success to the North British Railway Company and health to you and yours.'

Dr John Inglis as well as being a director of the North British was head of the shipbuilding and engineering firm of A. & J. Inglis, Pointhouse, Glasgow. His influence in the locomotive department had profound results for the NB. It was at his prompting that the company moved away from its traditional small engine policy and produced the Reid Atlantic.

George Johnstone was the son of the minister of the church in Springburn, Glasgow where James Reid, proprietor of Neilson & Co, and his family worshipped. His non-place in railway history depends on the fact that, as an inventor and experimenter with internal combustion engines, he tried to interest Reid in backing a motor car he had devised. Reid, steeped in steam as he was, saw no future in the motor car. Johnstone, in partnership with William Arrol went on to produce the successful Arrol-Johnstone car.

David Jones was an early English recruit to the Highland railway scene. In 1855 he made the surprising move from the Longsight works of the LNWR to the recently opened Inverness & Nairn Railway. He became locomotive superintendent of the Highland Railway in 1869 and proceeded to produce class after class of distinctive and efficient locomotives. He had been at Inverness 41 years when he was obliged to resign through ill health following an accident at work.

Li Hung Chang was perhaps the most colourful of the many customers who came to Glasgow to buy locomotives. A Chinese potentate of great power, he arrived in 1896 with a large retinue, attired in brightly-coloured Oriental costumes. The Hyde Park hierarchy, not to be outdone, accompanied the visitors on their tour of the works in full morning dress.

James Manson began his apprenticeship at the Glasgow & South Western Railway works, Kilmarnock, in 1861. He duly graduated from the engineering shops to the drawing office, but soon abandoned railway engineering for marine engineering. A spell with Barclay, Curle & Co on the Clyde was followed by service as a third, second and chief engineer on foreign-going vessels. By 1875 a very experienced Manson was back at Kilmarnock as works manager. In 1883 he became locomotive superintendent of the Great North of Scotland Railway where his managerial as well as his technical ability breathed new life into the locomotive department. In 1890 Manson returned to the G & SW as locomotive superintendent, a position he filled with distinction for 22 years.

Donald A. Matheson served on the London & North Western Railway and was chief assistant to the engineer of the Lancashire & Yorkshire Railway before joining the Caledonian as resident engineer during the construction of the Glasgow Central underground line. Subsequently he became engineer in chief of the company. The Caledonian sent him on a study tour of American railways. He was awarded the James Watt and George Stephenson gold medals of the Institution of Civil Engineers. In 1910 he was made general manager of the Caledonian.

James Miller was Scotland's foremost railway architect. Among the buildings he designed were Turnberry Hotel, the extension of Glasgow Central station and Wemyss Bay and Botanic Gardens stations. A large hotel designed by Miller for the G & SW at Princes Pier was not proceeded with. Like Charles Rennie Macintosh, Miller designed the interior fittings and furniture of his hotels. One of his finest buildings was the head office of the North British Locomotive Company Ltd, now the Springburn College of Engineering.

Norman Doran Macdonald was a flamboyant Victorian criminal lawyer who went train spotting in top hat and tails. Still in the files of the North British Railway is a letter he wrote to the general manager of the company explaining in detail what steps he should take to ensure winning the 1895 races for the East Coast group of companies. He conducted a group of North Eastern Railway officials on a study tour of American railways although he himself had never set foot in the country, and he publicly claimed to have 'assisted Mr McIntosh' with the design of the Dunalastair.

Robert McAlpine, a bricklayer's labourer, went into business for himself as a small builder, his first contract being 'signal houses' for the Glasgow, Bothwell, Hamilton & Coatbridge Railway. He very soon graduated to building entire

J F McIntosh (with rosette), locomotive superintendent of the
Caledonian Railway, at Carlisle on the day of the great Caledonian
employees excursion in 1899, in which 14,000 people took part.

railways including the Lanarkshire & Ayrshire
and the Lanarkshire & Dumbartonshire. On the
Mallaig Extension of the West Highland Railway he was known as Concrete Bob because of
his imaginative use of mass concrete in bridge
construction.

John Farquharson McIntosh, a former engine
driver with the Scottish North Eastern Railway
was promoted from the ranks to be locomotive
superintendent of the Caledonian Railway. His
Dunalastair brought him early fame. 'He is a
man of massive and powerful physique and is in
the very prime of life,' commented a Glasgow
periodical. He was a practical locomotive man
who knew just what his drivers wanted.

James McLeod in 1921 persuaded the North
British Locomotive Company to use the frames
and boiler of the Ramsay engine to produce a
condensing 4–4–0 + 0–4–4 geared steam turbine
locomotive. The NBL saw a future for the engine
in the export trade to waterless countries and
made it the key exhibit at their stand at the
British Empire Exhibition at Wembley in 1924.
But the engine failed to find favour with railway
managements and was subsequently dismantled.

Walter Montgomerie Neilson recognised at an
early date that locomotive building was a growth
industry. By 1860 his small but highly successful
factory at Stobcross, Glasgow was unable to

cope with orders and he established the Hyde
Park Works of Neilson & Co at the same time
taking on James Reid as managing partner. Neilson was a superb engineer but no businessman.
The deed of partnership was so drawn that Reid
had an option in 20 years time to acquire sole interest in the works. Neilson allowed himself to be
tricked out of the firm his family had founded
and bore his name. 'He took every shilling out of
my pocket that it was possible for him to do,'
wrote Neilson of Reid. From 1883 Reid became
sole proprietor of Neilson & Co. Neilson set up a
brand new works adjacent to Hyde Park in 1884,
but by 1888 the firm, the Clyde Locomotive
Company, was in financial difficulties and was
bought up by Sharp, Stewart & Co Ltd as their
Atlas Works.

William Paton was the first locomotive superintendent of the Edinburgh & Glasgow Railway,
and built the first locomotives turned out of
Cowlairs Works. When a passenger was killed as
the result of a mechanical defect in a locomotive
Paton was held personally responsible for his
death, and was jailed for a year. On his release
his drivers and firemen conducted him, with
band playing, from the prison gates to a Glasgow hostelry for a banquet in his honour.

Robert Band Pope, who worked for Neilson &
Co in the early days, is said to have been the first
man to suggest that locomotives be provided
with protective cabs.

The Duke of Portland introduced the first steam locomotive to Scotland, and was the first person to give George Stephenson substantial encouragement. The engine was not a success because of the unsuitable nature of the track of the Duke's Kilmarnock & Troon Railway.

D. McNab Ramsay, of the Ramsay Condensing Locomotive Co Ltd of Glasgow, in 1909 built at the Hyde Park Works of the North British Locomotive Company in co-operation with the proprietors, a turbine condensing locomotive with electric transmission. The engine had a box style appearance with all mechanical parts, coal bunkers and tanks enclosed. Superheated steam drove the turbine generator at 3000 rpm, current being supplied to four traction motors. The engine ran trials on the Caledonian and North British before being laid up at Hyde Park.

James Reid was discovered by Walter Neilson when he was a young draughtsman at the shipyard of Caird & Co of Greenock. Neilson took him under his wing at his Stobcross Works where he eventually became manager. After a short spell with Sharp Stewart & Co Ltd in Manchester Reid returned to Neilson & Co as described above. The Reid family remained in sole control of Hyde Park Works until 1903, when the firm combined with Sharp Stewart & Co and Dübs' Glasgow Locomotive Works to form the North British Locomotive Company Ltd. A statue of James Reid still stands in Springburn Park, Glasgow not far from the site of the works.

William Paton Reid, locomotive superintendent of the North British was a direct descendant of William Paton the first incumbent at Cowlairs. He is best remembered for his NB Atlantics.

Andrew Robertson, an itinerant Scottish teacher, encountered the young George Stephenson by accident in 1799 and taught him arithmetic. Stephenson proved an apt pupil, covering the normal four or five year course in a few months. When Stephenson moved to a new pit Robertson moved with him.

Edward Snowball was born in Northumberland about the same time as the first locomotives. He served an apprenticeship with Robert Stephenson and became chief draughtsman of Neilson & Co in 1862, a position he was to hold for 38 years. He it was who, over the years, gave the Neilson engine its distinctive character.

George Stephenson in his youth was employed for a time as an engine wright in a mill at Montrose. On his return to Northumberland he was impressed to fight in the Napoleonic wars and he used his Scottish earnings to pay for a substitute to take his place. Had he not had the money railway history might well have been different.

Robert Stephenson was educated at Edinburgh University. While a student there he sent notes of his lectures to his father so that he could benefit from them. George Stephenson, in a letter to his friend Mr Locke, said of his son, 'I have had him educated in the first Schools and is now in Collidge (sic) in Edinbro.'

Robert Louis Stevenson was a keen railway traveller. 'There are many ways of seeing landscape,' he wrote, 'and none more vivid in spite of canting dilettantes than from a railway train.'

Patrick Stirling bore one of the great names in British locomotive history. He received his initial training in the family works in Dundee and added to his skills with a spell as locomotive superintendent of the Caledonian & Dumbartonshire and service with Neilson & Co and Hawthorn of Newcastle, before becoming locomotive superintendent of the G & SW at the age of 33. In 1866 he landed the plum job of locomotive superintendent of the Great Northern

James Stirling who had served under his brother at Kilmarnock succeeded him as G & SW locomotive superintendent on his departure for the south. James, following in his brother's footsteps, eventually became locomotive superintendent of the South Eastern Railway.

William Stroudley made his name in Scotland. He was works manager at Cowlairs in Edinburgh & Glasgow days before transferring to the Highland Railway as that company's first locomotive superintendent. He designed the first three engines built in the company's Lochgorm works, and produced snowploughs and devised a technique for fighting the snowblocks which plagued the system. He left the Highland reluctantly in 1869, following a dispute about salary, to take up the locomotive superintendency of the London, Brighton & South Coast Railway.

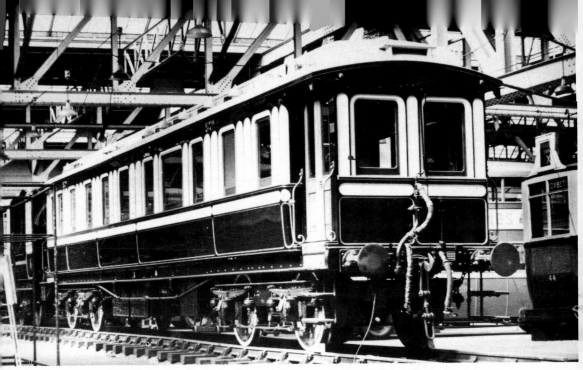

The Duke of Sutherland's bogie saloon, built at Wolverton in 1900 and today preserved as part of the National Collection at York. His engine and four-wheel saloon are preserved in Canada.

The Duke of Sutherland built at his own expense a line 18 miles long from Golspie to Helmsdale. At first isolated from the rest of the system the Duke operated a service over his line between Dunrobin, his residence, and a point near Helmsdale, using his own engine and driver. The line eventually became part of the Highland's far north route. Following the death of the Duke in 1892 his son acquired a new engine named *Dunrobin* for his own use and for the conveyance of his guests north of Inverness. A panel in the cab was inscribed with the names of distinguished passengers. The engine is now in Canada.

Sir James Thompson was born at Kirtlebridge and as a boy saw the navvies at work building the main line of the Caledonian outside his door. When the line was opened from Beattock to Carlisle in September 1847 he joined the company as an office boy. Fifty years later he was general manager of the Caledonian and in that year he became the first Scottish railway manager to be knighted. We are told of Sir James that 'his household talk is garnished and illustrated with phrases employed by the National Bard.'

John Wordie came from an old carting family that refused to accept ruin when the railway came. Realising that trains could not go up streets or along country lanes, Wordie organised a network of railway carts that would convey goods from station to customer and founded a great business in the process.

KEY DATES IN SCOTTISH RAILWAY HISTORY

6 July 1812	Kilmarnock & Troon Railway opened. It was a mineral line using horse haulage although a locomotive was tried unsuccessfully about 1817. Passengers were carried irregularly and unofficially.
1 October 1826	Monkland & Kirkintilloch Railway opened. This was a mineral railway designed to transport coal from the Monklands to the Forth & Clyde Canal basin at Kirkintilloch. Although the Act authorising the railway was the first ever to specify the use of steam locomotives, horse haulage was used until 10 May 1831 when a Glasgow-built locomotive was introduced.

June 1831	Garnkirk & Glasgow Railway opened. This was the first public passenger-carrying railway in Scotland. Two Stephenson-built locomotives were employed. The Glasgow terminus was at Glebe Street, Townhead. (The ceremonial opening of the line took place on 27 September 1831.)
July 1831	Edinburgh & Dalkeith Railway opened. It was horse operated and carried passengers and goods. The Edinburgh terminus was at St Leonards.
December 1831	Dundee & Newtyle Railway opened. The main purpose of the railway was to bring the agricultural produce of Strathmore to Dundee and return coal and lime to Strathmore. Horse haulage was used on level stretches and rope haulage with stationary steam engines on the inclines.
21 July 1840	Glasgow–Ayr line opened throughout.
12 August 1840	Bridge Street station, Glasgow, opened.
March 1841	Glasgow–Greenock line opened. First integrated train and steamer service to Clyde resorts.
22 February 1842	Edinburgh & Glasgow Railway opened. Queen Street station, Glasgow, and Haymarket station, Edinburgh, brought into use.
18 June 1846	North British Railway opened from North Bridge (later Waverley station) Edinburgh to Berwick-on-Tweed with a branch to Haddington. A coach link from Berwick to Newcastle provided a rail connection to London.
15 February 1848	Caledonian Railway opened from Carlisle to Glasgow and Edinburgh. First through service without change of carriage between London and the Scottish cities. The trains ran to Townhead station, Glasgow, and Lothian Road, Edinburgh.
7 August 1848	Caledonian Railway linked to the Scottish Central Railway at Castlecary. Through rail communication established between London and Perth.
1 November 1849	Buchanan Street station, Glasgow, opened. This station now became the terminus for the Anglo-Scottish trains and remained so until the opening of the Central station.
April 1850	Aberdeen Railway opened. Through communication established between London and Aberdeen.
29 August 1850	Royal Border Bridge across the Tweed at Berwick opened. First through trains between London and Edinburgh by the East Coast route.
28 October 1850	Glasgow & South Western Railway formed by the amalgamation of the Glasgow, Paisley, Kilmarnock & Ayr Railway and the Glasgow, Dumfries & Carlisle Railway. Through communication between Glasgow and Carlisle via Nithsdale commenced.
10 August 1852	The Morayshire Railway, first railway north of the Grampians, opened between Elgin and Lossiemouth.
20 August 1854	Great North of Scotland Railway opened from Kittybrewster (Aberdeen) to Huntly.
6 November 1855	Inverness & Nairn Railway opened.
1 April 1856	Waterloo station, Aberdeen, opened for passenger traffic.
31 May 1858	Glasgow–Helensburgh line opened.
18 August 1858	Through communication opened between Aberdeen and Inverness.
24 May 1860	The railway reaches Girvan.
12 March 1861	Portpatrick Railway opened from Castle Douglas to Stranraer.
1 July 1862	Waverley Route opened. (Opened for goods 24 June 1862). Through communication between Edinburgh and Carlisle via Hawick.
3 July 1862	Railway reaches Peterhead.
9 September 1863	Through direct communication established between Inverness and Perth.
24 April 1865	Railway reaches Fraserburgh.
29 June 1865	Highland Railway formed by amalgamation of Inverness & Perth Junction Railway and the Inverness & Aberdeen Junction Railway.
4 November 1867	Denburn Valley line links Kittybrewster to the new Joint station at Aberdeen.
2 May 1870	Princes Street station, Edinburgh, opened. (Station completed 1894.)

19 August 1870	Railway reaches Strome Ferry. (Dingwall & Skye line.)
1 April 1871	College station, Glasgow, opened. This station was used by certain suburban trains and by trains to Edinburgh via Bathgate. When the Glasgow City & District Railway (Queen Street Low Level line) was opened on 15 March 1886 High Street station superseded College.
2 April 1873	The first sleeping car service in Britain was inaugurated by the North British Railway on this date between Glasgow (Queen Street) and London (King's Cross) using a sleeping car built as a speculation by the Ashbury Railway Carriage and Iron Company. The public did not take readily to the idea of sleeping on wheels. By October the carriage was running with 0.9 of a passenger per journey.
28 July 1874	Railway reaches Wick and Thurso.
1 May 1876	On this day St Enoch station, Glasgow, was opened and the Midland route from Glasgow and Edinburgh Waverley to London St Pancras via Settle was inaugurated.
1 June 1878	Tay Bridge opened to the public.
1 August 1879	Central station, Glasgow, opened.
28 December 1879	Tay Bridge collapsed in storm.
1 July 1880	Railway opened to Oban.
15 May 1882	Craigendoran pier opened.
1 December 1884	Edinburgh Suburban line opened.
1 June 1885	Railway reaches Largs.
20 April 1887	Second Tay Bridge brought into use.

SCOTTISH RAILWAY STATISTICS 1913

LINE & FINANCE / PASSENGER TRAFFIC

	Route miles (including lines leased or worked)		Capital	Carriages owned	Passengers Carried	Season tickets
	(m)	(ch)	(£)			
Caledonian	1,117	59	70,910,471	2,242	47,505,472	32,428
Campbeltown & Machrihanish	6	29	29,304	6	107,012	2
Glasgow & South Western	491	72	24,934,056	1,179	18,672,560	10,359
Glasgow District Subway	6	44	1,331,850	52	14,574,334	—
Great North of Scotland	334	40	7,740,790	470	3,869,520	2,831
Highland	505	71	6,871,122	313	2,331,576	961
North British	1,375	64	66,895,769	2,623	43,141,196	24,873
Portpatrick & Wigtownshire Joint	41	11	491,980	—	458,236	160
Total	3,879	70	179,205,342	6,885	130,659,906	71,604

GOODS STOCK AND TRAFFIC

	Open	Wagons Covered	Mineral	Cattle	Others	Service
Caledonian	14,370	2,477	28,604	1,422	5,043	2,078
Campbeltown & Machrihanish						
Glasgow & South Western	3,680	1,097	11,986	660	1,538	1,315
Glasgow District Subway						
Great North of Scotland	2,918	372		265	107	1,104
Highland	1,799	188		292	262	108
North British	14,078	3,795	39,049	1,437	2,000	3,277
Portpatrick & Wigtownshire Joint						
Total	36,845	7,929	79,637	4,076	8,950	6,882

1 June 1889	Gourock station and pier opened.
4 March 1890	Forth Bridge opened by Prince of Wales.
2 April 1894	Cathcart Circle opened.
7 August 1894	West Highland Railway opened from Craigendoran to Fort William.
10 August 1896	Glasgow Central (Low Level) and Glasgow Central Railway underground system opened.
2 November 1897	Dingwall & Skye line extended to Kyle of Lochalsh.
1 November 1898	Aviemore–Inverness direct line opened.
1 April 1901	West Highland Railway extended to Mallaig.
31 October 1908	Rope haulage on Cowlairs Incline discontinued.
22 May 1915	Troop train disaster at Quintinshill (Gretna), 224 killed.
1 May 1928	First Edinburgh–London non-stop run of *Flying Scotsman*.
5 November 1960	Glasgow (north bank) electrification inaugurated. Steam services were resumed on 19 December following a defect in the electrical equipment.
10 September 1962	Edinburgh Suburban line closed to passengers.
14 June 1965	Dumfries–Stranraer line closed.
6 September 1965	Princes Street station, Edinburgh, closed.
27 June 1966	St Enoch station, Glasgow, closed.
7 November 1966	Buchanan Street station, Glasgow, closed.
4 June 1967	Perth–Aberdeen route via Forfar closed.
6 January 1969	Waverley Route closed.
5 May 1974	Inauguration of Glasgow–London electric service.

TRAFFIC RECEIPTS AND EXPENSES

Revenue			Expenses
Pass. Parcels Mail	Goods	Total	
(£)	(£)	(£)	(£)
2,094,440	2,975,466	5,069,906	3,049,591
1,947	920	2,867	2,306
902,000	1,079,029	1,981,029	1,248,965
56,215	—	56,215	37,411
272,376	254,439	517,815	281,769
369,461	221,469	590,930	345,344
1,961,984	3,240,837	5,202,821	3,010,741
36,589	23,911	60,500	50,433
5,695,012	7,787,071	13,482,083	8,026,560

Total	Goods Carried (Tons)	Minerals (Tons)	Livestock
53,994	6,108,313	22,194,749	1,950,284
		29,591	
20,276	2,088,360	7,241,259	1,226,124
3,766	567,377	474,313	375,933
2,649	346,502	319,685	621,577
63,636	6,738,818	26,434,331	2,743,494
	70,355	94,535	177,604
144,321	15,919,725	56,788,463	7,095,016

ACKNOWLEDGEMENTS

As always the Scottish Record Office provided a wealth of source material both for the text and illustrative matter in this book. I am indebted to the Keeper of the Records of Scotland and his staff for the superb service rendered, and especially to the always helpful George Barbour. Documents created by the railway companies are reproduced with the approval of the Keeper of the Records of Scotland. Thanks are due also to Murdoch Nicholson of the Mitchell Library, Glasgow and Don Martin of Strathkelvin District Library for their assistance in locating interesting material.

Illustrations not from the author's collection or that of Locomotive & General Railway Photographs are:

Isaac Black 45 (top); W.E. Boyd 14; British Rail 74 (bottom), 80; Dr W.R. Brown 51 (top), 64 (bottom), 67; A.G. Dunbar 18, 48, (bottom right), 61 (top, bottom); John Goss 83; M. Halbert 59 (top); G.T. Heavyside 20; G.M. Kichenside 92; Kirkintilloch Camera Club 44; Mitchell Library 70, 71, 72, 73, 74 (top), 75; A.A. Maclean 17; G. & D. McCrory 62 (bottom); J.F. McEwan 62 (top left); D.W. McMillan 46 (bottom), 59 (bottom), 96; H.J. Patterson Rutherford 24 (top); Scottish Record Office 6, 7, 26 (top), 31, 32, 33, 37, 42, 43 (top), 45 (bottom), 46 (top, middle), 47 (bottom), 48 (top), 56 (bottom), 58, 60, 63, 77, 90; Donald Stuart 52; Jack Templeton 57; W.S. Thomson 69.

Caledonian West Coast route express headed by 4–4–0 No 888, one of J F McIntosh's 900 class.

LOCOMOTIVES AND ROAD VEHICLES

	Tender	Tank	Total	Rail motors	Road vehicles (Passenger)	Road vehicles (Goods)	Engine Mileage
Caledonian	609	388	997	1	1	1,006	27,886,220
Campbeltown & Machrihanish		3	3				24,218
Glasgow & South Western	486	35	521	3		684	12,232,914
Glasgow District Subway							1,194,230*
Great North of Scotland	97	20	117		35	8	2,835,159
Highland	125	28	153			1	3,869,486
North British	726	332	1,058				29,571,648
Portpatrick & Wigtownshire Joint							
Total	2,043	806	2,849	4	36	1,699	77,613,875

* Cable hauled

REVENUE AND EXPENSE STATISTICS 1912

	Passenger rev. per train mile	Goods rev. per train mile	Percentage of expenses to receipts
Caledonian	47.77d	100.12d	59
North British	50.12d	86.67d	58
Glasgow & South Western	45.07d	87.09d	60

	PW maintenance per train mile	Locomotive power per train mile	Rolling stock repairs and renewals per train mile
Caledonian	7.14d	12.03d	4.84d
North British	6.57d	11.81d	4.43d
Glasgow & South Western	5.53d	11.05d	3.56d

COMPARATIVE STATISTICS 1912

	Scotland	England
No of locomotives per mile of track	.66	1.21
No of carriages per mile of track	1.58	2.76
No of wagons per mile of track	36.73	36.71
Average rate of dividend	3.07%	3.58%
Proportion of receipts from passenger trains	42%	46%
Total revenue per mile (All traffic)	£3,316	£6,211
Revenue per passenger train mile	46.26d	50.97d
Revenue per goods train mile	88.72d	103.49d
Cost of PW maintenance per train mile	6.27d	6.79d
Cost of locomotive power per train mile	11.45d	12.96d
Carriage and wagon renewals and repairs per train mile	4.09d	4.24d
Traffic expenses per train mile	11.17d	14.23d
For damage or loss of goods per train mile	.13d	.37d
Total working expenses per train mile	39.01d	45.83d